Treating the New Anxiety

Treating the New Anxiety

A Cognitive-Theological Approach

Kirk A. Bingaman

JASON ARONSON
Lanham • Boulder • New York • Toronto • Plymouth, UK

Published in the United States of America
by Jason Aronson
An imprint of Rowman & Littlefield Publishers, Inc.

A wholly owned subsidiary of
The Rowman & Littlefield Publishing Group, Inc.
4501 Forbes Boulevard, Suite 200, Lanham, Maryland 20706
www.rowmanlittlefield.com

Estover Road
Plymouth PL6 7PY
United Kingdom

British Library Cataloguing in Publication Information Available

Library of Congress Cataloging-in-Publication Data

Bingaman, Kirk A.
  Treating the new anxiety : a cognitive-theological approach / Kirk A. Bingaman.
    p. cm.
  Includes bibliographical references and index.
  ISBN-13: 978-0-7657-0462-7 (cloth : alk. paper)
  ISBN-10: 0-7657-0462-5 (cloth : alk. paper)
  ISBN-13: 978-0-7657-0463-4 (pbk. : alk. paper)
  ISBN-10: 0-7657-0463-3 (pbk. : alk. paper)
  1. Anxiety—Treatment. 2. Cognitive therapy. 3. Spiritual care (Medical care) I.
Title.

  RC531.B45 2007
  616.85'2206—dc22   2007017300

Printed in the United States of America

⊗™ The paper used in this publication meets the minimum requirements of
American National Standard for Information Sciences—Permanence of Paper
for Printed Library Materials, ANSI/NISO Z39.48-1992.

TO ANNIE

who gives meaning to my life

Contents

~

Acknowledgments

I am indebted to my colleagues in the Graduate School of Religion and Religious Education (GSRRE) at Fordham University. This project had its inception at the GSRRE doctoral colloquium in the fall of 2005, where I was invited to be the keynote presenter. I am grateful to the dean of the GSRRE, Fr. Anthony Ciorra, for his continued support and encouragement, to associate dean, Bert Binder, and to the faculty: Drs. Claudio Burgaleta, Lisa Cataldo, Gloria Durka, John Elias, Harold Horell, German Martinez, Beverly Musgrave, Janet Ruffing, and Kieran Scott.

I am grateful to Dr. Warren Tryon of the Psychology Department at Fordham University for his elucidation of *automaticity*, or automatic processing, and for the conversations about the application of cognitive–behavioral therapy to the religious and theological beliefs of clients and to the treatment of anxiety. Sr. Ellen Dauwer patiently answered my numerous questions about technology.

I am grateful to the Office of Sponsored Programs at Fordham University, which awarded me a grant for this project. The grant covered the work of my research assistant, Danielle DeSaro, who worked diligently with me. I am also grateful for the help of my GSRRE student assistants Linda Capobianco and Maritza Ortiz Cruz.

The writing life is a particularly solitary endeavor, and it is therefore important to have friends and communities of support along the way. I am grateful to the Reverend Leslie Mott and members of the congregation of First Presbyterian Church in Cold Spring, New York, for their encouragement and curiosity about the project.

x ～ Acknowledgments

Finally, I am grateful to the staff of Rowman & Littlefield Publishers, for their generous assistance with this project: Dr. Arthur Pomponio, editorial director, for his important feedback by way of numerous emails and telephone conversations; Mary Catherine La Mar, editorial assistant, for her thoughtful comments and suggestions; Melissa McNitt, production editor, for her guidance with the production process; and Alla Corey, marketing manager, for her help with publicity.

~

What Is Prompting
the New Anxiety?

Fears are educated into us and can, if we wish, be educated out.

—Karl Menninger

Americans are anxious. To a certain extent, it has always been this way: The Civil War pushed the country to the precipice of dissolution; the Great Depression bankrupted many individuals, families, and businesses, from which some never recovered; the World Wars sobered the nation up to the reality that human beings may not be so enlightened after all; and the tumultuous 1960s, characterized by deep divisions over race, war, and the trustworthiness of government, challenged the idealism of "one nation under God." Thus, Americans are hardly strangers to living with anxiety. Likewise, those who care for Americans, be they psychotherapists, mental health practitioners, or pastoral counselors, have been dealing with anxiety all along. In other words, a case can be made that there is nothing new under the sun.

An equally compelling case can be made for the fact that Americans post–September 11 are living in a new age of anxiety. To be sure, someone who fell asleep à la Rip Van Winkle before September 11 and has now awakened to the new world may wonder what happened. For starters, Americans now realize that they are no longer immune to terrorism. Before, we could see acts of terrorism reported on the evening news, but these violent actions were always far removed, geographically "over there" in some distant part of the world. Now, we are all too aware that acts of terrorism can be perpetrated anywhere and at anytime, even in America on a gloriously beautiful September morning. We may not dwell on this consciously, yet we need only look to Freud to be reminded that anticipatory anxiety can still be gnawing away in the deep recesses of the unconscious. But even if we attempt to repress our vulnerability, as individuals and as a nation, there is always nighttime cable news to keep the dangers of the post–September 11 world ever before us ad infinitum.

Frank Furedi (2005), a sociologist at the University of Kent, points out "that many people believe they live in frightening times because other people want them to feel that way." This would most certainly apply to nighttime cable news, which stays in business to the extent that they can get us to buy into the premise that the times in which we live are uniquely dangerous and frightening—the better to keep members of the viewing audience on the edge of their seats and therefore glued to the television sets where each evening they get a full and complete recap of clear and present dangers as well as potential dangers that are lurking on the not-too-distant horizon. One reason why we are so anxious and fearful is that these "fear entrepreneurs" sell us their product through scare tactics:

> Politicians, the media, businesses, environmental organizations, public health officials and advocacy groups are continually warning us about something new to fear. . . . The activities of these fear entrepreneurs serve to transform our anxieties about life into tangible fears. Every major event becomes the focus for competing claims about what you need to fear.

Furedi sees an alternative to this climate of anxiety and fear:

> The precondition for effectively countering the politics of fear is to challenge the association of personhood with the state of vulnerability. Anxieties about uncertainty become magnified and overwhelm us when we regard ourselves as essentially vulnerable. Yet the human imagination possesses a formidable capacity to engage and learn from the risks it faces. There is always an alternative. Whether or not we are aware of the choices confronting us depends upon whether we regard ourselves as defined by our vulnerability or by our capacity to be resilient. (p. 3)

Challenging the association of personhood with the state of vulnerability is addressed in coming chapters. For now, suffice it to say that Furedi (2005) has his finger on the pulse of Western society and that what he writes certainly captures the anxious mood of many Americans. Anxiety and fear are hot commodities, as illustrated by the preponderance of fear entrepreneurs.

We have already identified the media as agents of fear, most notably in the form of nighttime cable television news. There are, however, as Furedi makes clear, other fear entrepreneurs who capitalize on the anxiety and vulnerability of Americans. Take politicians, for example. Since September 11, the political rhetoric has focused to a large extent on America's sense of anxiety, vulnerability, and victimization but in ways that are quite different from those of the past. Americans, as I stated earlier, have lived through anxious times before. But what is missing from the political rhetoric post–September 11 is a sense of hope and resilience. Franklin Roosevelt's "The only thing we have to fear is fear itself," John F. Kennedy's "Ask what you can do for your country," and even Ronald Reagan's reference to America as "a shining city on a hill," all conveying the spirit of hope and resilience, have given way to a politics of vulnerability and victimization. Americans feel anxious and vulnerable, and supposedly to bolster our confidence, we hear our elected officials assure us that they intend to keep America safe by, for example, stemming the flow of illegal immigration and taking the war to the terrorists in such locations as Afghanistan and Iraq. And yet, the politics of fear do little to make Americans feel more hopeful and less anxious. They are designed to keep political fear entrepreneurs in elected office, pure and simple.

Not that the new anxiety that Americans are experiencing is entirely a figment of imagination. The coordinated terrorist attack on September 11, 2001, in New York, Washington, and the fields of Pennsylvania was very real, as is the potential for future terrorist attacks on American soil. Moreover, the images and recorded messages from Al-Jazeera that we see and hear on our televisions and computers seem to reinforce the potential for and inevitability of future terrorist acts. It is, in other words, not a matter of if but when. Americans can strive to be brave and resilient in the face of this potential danger, yet at the same time it is quite understandable if we still feel somewhat anxious and vulnerable. From a sociological standpoint, maybe we can define the choice as one or the other, as either-or: We regard ourselves as being defined by our vulnerability or by our capacity to be resilient. But, if we view the present situation through other lenses, say, psychological and theological, we begin to see more of the complexities inherent in the human heart and mind. In an age of anxiety, the choice is not simply to regard ourselves as being defined by our vulnerability or by our capacity to be resilient. Rather, the more fundamental issue is defining ourselves as being genuinely hopeful and resilient, our anxiety and vulnerability notwithstanding. To assist us in finding authentic hope and meaning in an age of anxiety, I look toward theology as a resource to apply to our lives as caregivers and to the lives of anxious clients in our care.

Beyond the more obvious effects of post–September 11 living, there are other developments that are cause for concern. Furedi (2005) cites environmental organizations and health officials as part of the fear entrepreneurs, yet there are certain environmental issues and health matters that make us more than a little anxious—and rightly so. We have been hearing the scientific community, more and more in a voice of unanimity, issue forth a warning about the effects of climate change on a global scale. Although those in government may or may not be responsive to the scientific data on global warming, there is mounting evidence to suggest that if we soon do not find alternative energy resources, above and beyond fossil fuels, then the planet in the not-too-distant future will pass the point of no return. And this is even without factoring into the equation the more cutting-edge scientific research that focuses on not merely the phenomenon of global warming caused by the release of massive amounts of carbon emissions into the atmosphere but on that of global dimming caused by the accumulation of vast quantities of dirty particles into the earth's atmosphere. Combined, global warming and global dimming are leading more than a few scientists to conclude that if we do not change course in the next few decades or even reverse course, then the world that we bequeath to our children and to their children will be one that does not leave them better off but rather in a more precarious position.

In addition, it now appears as if the world is about to reach or has already reached its peak in terms of the discovery of potential oil fields. As reported in the fall of 2005 in *The New York Times Magazine*, we have begun to witness "the beginning of the end of oil" (cover; see Maass, 2005). Not that the world is about to run out of oil anytime soon. There is, however, some consensus that we have reached a worldwide peak with oil discovery and production, from which we will be on the downward slope in the next few decades. Unless we manage to reduce our reliance as a nation and as a world on fossil fuels, the future becomes rather ambiguous for the next generation and beyond. By the time that my own daughter reaches my age, three decades from now, America as well as other nations of the world will need to be far less reliant on oil. If not, if nations such as the United States and China are still more or less dependent on fossil fuels for energy, then it can only portend turf battles for the limited amount of oil that remains.

There is, then, nothing new under the sun, in the sense that human beings have had to deal with anxiety from time immemorial. Moreover, anxiety, as I have already noted, is hardly a new phenomenon when it comes to America. Sill, there is a certain uniqueness about the anxiety post–September 11. Further terrorism aimed at Americans appears highly inevitable, as a reprisal for our invasion of foreign countries. The earth warms and dims simultaneously, the result being that it is anyone's guess what the global atmosphere will be like 50 years from now. In any case, the majority of scientific scenarios are not encouraging, and the reality of what we must grapple with immediately can only be repressed for so long. As Freud pointed out so seminally, the repressed can only remain repressed for so long, until that which is repressed resurfaces, in this context, in the form of anxiety about the future of the country and of the world.

To some extent, the anxiety that is being experienced by Americans at present has to do with trying to differentiate between the entrepreneurs who attempt to sell us fear and the more enlightened voices who are simply identifying legitimate concerns. This ambiguity can be seen in the context of how we approach the thorny issue of immigration. For some, particularly for fear entrepreneurs—most notably, those who appear on nighttime cable television—illegal immigration symbolizes the decline of American strength and homogeneity. What exacerbates this fear is that the new immigrants, legal or not, are different from previous immigrants who gladly assimilated into homogenous American life and culture. In contrast, new immigrants wish to retain their cultural heritage. How these diverse cultural and ethnic groups maintain their original identity while assimilating into American society is not altogether clear. Nor can we look to Europe for any guidance in how to balance assimilation and multiculturalism, because, as David Rieff (2005) argues in *The New York Times Magazine*,

> the European vision of multiculturalism, in all its simultaneous good will and self-congratulation, is no longer sustainable. And most Europeans know it. . . . It makes all of Europe's other problems, from the economy to the euro to the sclerosis of social democracy, seem trivial by comparison. Unfortunately, unlike these challenges, this one is existential and urgent and has no obvious answer. (pp. 11–12)

Furthermore, David Brooks (2005), a *New York Times* columnist, believes that "countries that do not encourage assimilation are not only causing themselves trouble, but endangering others around the world as well" (p. A-19).

To merely write off Rieff and Brooks as fear entrepreneurs would be overly simplistic. How and, ultimately, if America can assimilate the new wave of culturally and ethnically diverse groups of people remains to be seen, especially in light of the emerging minority-to-majority demographics. Even if we do not regard ourselves as being defined by our vulnerability, there are perplexing issues post–September 11 that elicit in all of us more than a little anxiety. The world has changed and continues to change right before our eyes, seemingly on a daily basis. Moreover, the country is and will continue to be deeply divided over how best to respond to the inherently complex issues of immigration, pluralism, multiculturalism, and assimilation. Nor are we even remotely united in how we go about responding to the ongoing threat of terrorism, global warming and dimming, the inevitable end of oil later this century, and the urgent need to develop alternative sources of energy. And this is even without bringing into the discussion the impact of the so-called culture wars that divide Americans even further and show little sign of abating anytime soon. We lack a consensus for what constitutes American morality, particularly when it comes to issues such as family values, abortion, and human sexuality and sexual orientation.

But this is not all or maybe even the most potentially divisive issues confronting Americans at the present. There is also the matter of economics, specifically, the widening gap between the haves and the have-nots and the gradual disappearance of the American middle class as we know it. Heretofore, members of the middle class of American society could plan on steady employment from the time they left high school or college to the time they reached retirement. Additionally, they could rest assured that a pension awaited them at the point of retirement, which, along with Social Security, would sustain them financially for the rest of their lives. Not so anymore. For many have-nots and even a growing number of middle-class haves, the future is becoming increasingly unpredictable. The days of leaving high school or college and working for the "company" until age 65, a central component of life cycle theory for much of the past century, has little relevance in today's post–September 11 world. All the while, the wealthiest of Americans have managed to secure their status as the haves, an issue of justice that must be addressed not only theologically, from the pulpit in American churches, but also psychologically, in the context of psychotherapy, mental health counseling, and pastoral counseling. The issue of the application of theology to the context of caring for the anxious is revisited in greater detail in later chapters. For now, it is important to keep in mind that along with the anxiety associated with terrorism, global warming, the end of oil, and issues having to do with immigration and assimilation, the deeper anxiety in today's post–September 11 world could very well have more to do with the radically different landscape of American employment, the dangerously widening gap between the haves and the have-nots, and the vanishing middle class.

What is important to notice is the way in which certain issues that make us anxious have a tendency to be mutually reinforcing. The dramatic changes affecting, for example, American car manufacturers trigger anxiety in the rank and file of the automobile industry. Then the anxiety becomes exacerbated when automobile employees, already feeling enough stress to begin with from potential layoffs and the reduction in or elimination of their pensions, hear any hint of potential outsourcing. From a business standpoint, the jury seems to be out on whether outsourcing is merely a form of obtaining cheap labor or whether it is necessary to stay competitive in a global market. To the blue-collar laborer at General Motors, Ford, or Chrysler, whose employment and retirement status seemingly hang in the balance, it really makes little difference. Merely hearing the word *outsourcing* triggers feelings of anxiety, disappointment, and frustration, as does hearing the word *immigration* for those employed in the Southwest or California. Again, whether there is a correlation between immigration, even illegal immigration, and the actual loss of someone's job, there is still the perception among many Americans, often fueled by the fear entrepreneurs who appear nightly on cable television, that immigrants are coming to get our jobs.

That our anxiety becomes triggered and manipulated by the media is hardly surprising. Those who sell fear in the media stay on television to the extent that they get us to buy into their product—in this case, fear. Indeed, if more Americans were self-disciplined enough to turn off the television or to change the channel when they hear fear mongering coming from the talking heads, it would do wonders for their mental health by making them feel less anxious. But this may be wishful thinking, considering the pervasiveness of technology and the vast reach of the media juggernaut. Marc Augé (1995), the French anthropologist whose research involves the phenomena of supermodernity and nonplaces (which I apply extensively to the "new anxiety," in the next chapter), argues that what we are witnessing is seemingly an acceleration and overabundance of current events and world affairs. That these events seem to appear on an unprecedented scale is, according to Augé, "a by-product of technology." Said another way, this acceleration and overabundance of events, a by-product of the ubiquity of technology and media, "can be properly appreciated only by bearing in mind both our overabundant information and the growing tangle of interdependencies in what some already call the world system" (p. 28).

Technology is then a distinctly double-edged phenomenon. On one hand, it has the capacity to make our lives easier by offering to more and more of us the modern conveniences of life. On the other hand, technology has the capacity to make us more anxious and bewildered. As more people have access to personal computers, the Internet, cell phones, iPods, cable television, and air travel to other parts of the world, there will be, as Augé (1995) points out, an acceleration and multiplication of national and world events manifested in an overabundance of information. This presents us with a formidable challenge because the human brain is capable of absorbing only so much information, let alone processing it in any sort of meaningful and systematic way. Add to this the unceasing commentary on the overabundant events and information that we see and hear nightly on cable television and anytime on Internet home pages and blog sites, and we have a situation that leaves us feeling even more anxious as we futilely attempt to stay abreast of and find meaning in a world that keeps passing us by. Again, the issue of anxious living in a supermodern world is addressed more extensively in the next chapter.

A Methodological Framework

We could easily conclude that we are living in an age of considerable anxiety, and, as I have been noting, there is ample evidence for this assessment. And yet, at the same time, we do not want to hastily and shortsightedly conclude that anxiety is more of an issue today than it has ever been before or ever will be again. To be human is to live with a certain amount of anxiety in every time and place and in every day and age. We are therefore obligated to concur with the words from the Judeo-Christian scriptures that there is really nothing new under the sun. Anxiety, in other words, is hardly a new phenomenon experienced by human beings. At the same time, I argue that because of the transitional nature of the post–September 11 world, more and more people are feeling anxiety evermore acutely. My focus, then, from a methodological standpoint, is twofold: caring for the anxious in general and caring for anxious post–September 11 clients in particular. Because of my background and work in the fields of theology, pastoral counseling, and mental health counseling, I have been developing a therapeutic approach that encourages practitioners—including, as might be expected, those working in the fields of pastoral counseling and spiritual care as well as those working out of a more secular framework in the fields of psychotherapy and mental health counseling—to take more seriously the theological views and beliefs of anxious clients. In an age of anxiety, what a client believes about God, religious faith, and the present and future state of the world has a significant impact on his or her growth and development. It is also a determinant of whether the client can approach life proactively with authentic hope or whether he or she lives his or her life defensively and regressively, swayed by the rantings and ravings of fear entrepreneurs.

In chapter 2, I situate the new age of anxiety into the context of other cultural developments. For some time, we have been hearing that the modern age has given way to the postmodern era. Core beliefs and narratives that we had grounded our lives in before have been rigorously critiqued if not thoroughly deconstructed. We live, as it were, in a sort of wasteland of meaning, trying desperately at times to find some larger purpose in the momentous happenings going on right before our very eyes. But from the standpoint of postmodernism, there is no longer any ultimate meaning to be found, for we see what we want to see and we find what we want to find. Herein is the paradox: At the precise moment when we need to make sense of a rapidly changing nation and world, we are told by postmodernists that this is fundamentally impossible because absolute meaning derives from those who are in positions of power and such meaning is therefore ultimately self-serving. In other words, just when we need to examine our core beliefs and values to reconstruct fresh hope and meaning relevant to the present and future, we encounter, at every turn, the obstacle of postmodernism, which challenges every attempt at meaning making. Thus, as if life were not already challenging enough, we are expected, in the context of postmodernism, to resist the temptation to look for meaning where, supposedly, there is none. This has the intended effect of keeping us from imposing our political and theological views and narratives on other individuals and groups. At the same time, it leaves those already feeling anxious about the present and future states of the world even more anxious. The only recourse, it seems, by opting not to look for fresh meaning and timely relevant narratives, is to fall back on regressive beliefs and theologies that stymie rather than promote holistic growth and development.

Consequently, in chapter 2, I intentionally make a methodological and hermeneutical move in the direction of situating this study of the new anxiety in the context of not postmodernity but rather supermodernity. The two, as Augé (1995) clearly demonstrates, are not synonymous. If, for example, we focus on the exacerbation of anxiety by postmodernism, then we are forced to conclude that it is the collapse or the absence of any genuine meaning that makes those in our care feel more vulnerable. However, if we situate the present anxiety into the context of what Augé refers to as supermodernity, then what emerges is an anxiety intensified not so much by the nonexistence of meaning but rather by the acceleration of history and by the overabundance of current national and world events. The situation, instead of being defined vis-à-vis the postmodern collapse of meaning, is now viewed from the perspective of supermodernity, which holds that our anxiety is intensified because there is not enough time to attach meaning to current events and situations. It is not that meaning has completely collapsed or disappeared but rather that we are hard-pressed to attach any meaning to events and circumstances that are literally here today and gone tomorrow or maybe even gone the same day. The hermeneutical framework of trading postmodernity for supermodernity is less fatalistic and therefore potentially more hopeful.

In chapter 3, I focus on the nature of anxiety in general and the new anxiety in particular. I begin with an overview of the clinical criteria for anxiety as it is presented in the *Diagnostic and Statistical Manual of Mental Disorders* (2000, fourth edition, text revision; *DSM–IV–TR*) under the diagnosis *generalized anxiety disorder* (GAD). The hallmark of anxiety, or GAD, according to the *DSM–IV–TR*, is "excessive and uncontrollable worry" (as quoted in Rygh & Sanderson, 2004, p. 1). Moreover, anxiety that reaches levels of clinical concern is, as Donald Capps (1999) points out, "disproportionate to environmental threats" that may or may not occur in the present or in the future. Anxiety, therefore, is anticipatory, an unconsciously preemptive strategy to maintain a semblance of control by heading potential threats off at the proverbial pass before they ever occur or become reality. At the risk of oversimplifying, "anxiety is an anticipatory emotion [that] is felt in anticipation of real or imagined future events" (p. 12). As such, I explore in greater depth and detail the clinical and diagnostic features of anxiety, again, as they are presented under the rubric of GAD.

At the same time, I juxtapose the clinical definition of anxiety as it is found in the *DSM–IV–TR* with the new anxiety that we are encountering in a post–September 11 world. To what extent are the two forms of anxiety—generalized anxiety and the new anxiety—the same or at least similar? To what extent are they different? What criteria do we use to distinguish generalized anxiety from a post–September 11 form of anxiety, assuming that there are certain differences between the two? Both, for example, are anticipatory, intended to head off preemptively or at least prepare for an oncoming threat or crisis. The difference between the two, I suggest, has to do with the proportionality or disproportionality of the anxiety to the perceived environmental threats and dangers. Generalized anxiety, on one hand, is recognized most notably by "the cardinal feature of . . . apprehensive expectation" (Barlow, 2002, p. 572), or excessive uncontrollable worry that is, as Capps (1999) points out, disproportionate to potential threats and dangers. In contrast, the new anxiety may or may not be proportionate to the possibility of further terrorism, global warming, the beginning of the end of oil, immigration and assimilation, the outsourcing of employment and labor, and the vanishing American middle class. A great deal of worry, or apprehensive expectation, characterizes the new anxiety, but it is not necessarily disproportionate to a nation and a world that are in a state of tremendous flux and transition. The threats and dangers that we are facing as a nation are urgent, as the fear entrepreneurs are only all too happy to remind us about on a daily basis. The fear entrepreneurs notwithstanding, the new anxiety may not be so disproportionate after all, particularly when we situate it into the context of supermodernity. With the acceleration of history and the overabundance of national and world events ever before our eyes, it is a supremely tall order to try to ascertain what percentage of post–September 11 anxiety is proportionate and what percentage is not.

Additionally, in chapter 3, I discuss various therapeutic approaches to anxiety to determine the most effective form of care. It will become apparent that, as with generalized anxiety, the clear treatment of choice for the new anxiety is cognitive–behavioral therapy (CBT). With a proven track record, CBT is the psychosocial treatment that meets "criteria as an empirically supported treatment for [GAD]" (Rygh & Sanderson, 2004, p. 194). I extend these empirical findings to the treatment of the new anxiety.

Before going any further, however, I want to ask practitioners of other therapeutic approaches to bear with me, to suspend judgment until the end of this study, about the merits of cognitive therapy versus the merits of other psychotherapies. Personally, I am not a cognitive therapist; rather, I situate myself within a psychodynamic and family-systems framework. One colleague, a psychoanalyst, upon learning of my research, remarked, "Don't you worry that cognitive therapy doesn't do justice to the human person?" I remember thinking to myself that, of course, I am very much concerned about the depths of human personhood. At the same time, it has become imperative for practitioners at any time, but even more so in an age of heightened worry, to pay close attention to empirical research and findings. We may have, for example, an approach to therapy and counseling that works well in theory but is not that effective when applied to the clinical treatment of certain disorders. Whatever our therapeutic orientation, one must remember that with anxiety, CBT is clearly the treatment of choice. This is not to suggest that we all become cognitive therapists. What it does mean is that we give the application of cognitive therapy to the treatment of anxiety our open-minded consideration.

In chapter 4, I extend the findings that strongly suggest that CBT is the most efficacious form of treatment for generalized anxiety to the treatment of anxiety in a post–September 11 world. Indeed, the strength of CBT in treating anxiety is that it addresses, rather intentionally, cognitive responses to perceptions of threat in the form of images, thoughts, assumptions, and beliefs. "The beliefs . . . may be about the self, about others in relation to the self, and/or about worry or the problem-solving process" (Rygh & Sanderson, 2004, pp. 19, 84). But that is not all. If CBT is the treatment of choice when it comes to anxiety, then along with addressing beliefs about self, others, worry, and problem solving is the need to identify and address the anxious client's ontological beliefs, views, and images about God and ultimate reality.

As I argue later in the book, intentional exploration of the client's religious and theological beliefs and values is not optional in an age of anxiety. What the client believes about God and God's involvement in the world, both present and future, must be taken seriously. The power of religious and theological beliefs and values to shape our outlook about the present and future cannot be underestimated, nor can its power to ameliorate or exacerbate the anxious client's worry and apprehension.

Although the psychotherapeutic community has, in recent years, demonstrated a greater openness toward the religious, theological, and spiritual dimensions of human existence, there is still more than a little confusion over how practitioners go about engaging clients theologically in the counseling session. Some practitioners, of course, remain convinced that a client's belief system is off-limits in the context of therapy; it would be better, so the thinking goes, for the individual to discuss his or her religious beliefs and theological views with a priest, minister, or rabbi. In other words, let the clergy address matters theological while mental health professionals address issues of a psychological nature. And the twain, at least for some psychotherapists, shall never meet; or, if they do meet in the counseling session, better it be superficial. The psychotherapeutic ideal of neutrality, objectivity, and nondirectiveness still casts a rather long shadow over the profession, as if this modality is the most advantageous and beneficial form of care. It is rather ironic that in a profession that espouses the importance of integrative living, there has been a tendency to create a bifurcated framework for clients, essentially communicating to them that they are on their own when it comes to integrating their spirituality with other aspects of their lives.

This is most unfortunate and shortsighted, particularly when many of us are feeling so anxious. The need to help clients find new meaning, to help them reflect on what informs and sustains them theologically, is of the utmost importance in a time of great change and transition. Mental health practitioners simply cannot leave this dimension of human experience to clergy and professional theologians. American religion is in a tremendous state of flux. Although certain evangelical congregations and denominations would appear to be experiencing growth and vitality, others, such as Mainline Protestants, show steady signs of decline, as reflected in the annual loss of thousands of members. Even Roman Catholics who remain faithful to the church do so in a way that maintains a certain nuanced loyalty to their religious tradition; they belong to the church, but at a deeply personal level, they harbor theological views that are not necessarily in agreement with the official teaching of the church. The present situation is complicated even more by Americans' resistance to calling themselves *religious*, opting instead for the seemingly less-loaded term *spiritual*. Being spiritual, it should be noted, is a good thing. At the same time, contemporary spirituality has become an increasingly individualistic phenomenon, leaving many of us to find order, purpose, and meaning on our own. Contemporary spirituality, in many instances, lacks a communal connection, something vitally important at anytime but even more so when we are living in a time of great change. Thus, the new spirituality is rather double-edged: It is born out of a deep hunger and yearning to make sense of an increasingly complex world, yet because it often lacks a communal focus, it has the potential for making us feel alone, adrift, and therefore more anxious.

That contemporary spirituality has in many ways become unmoored from organized faith communities has important implications for practitioners caring for the anxious. For example, because the spiritual life is ultimately grounded in community and is thus not solipsistic, it begs the question, in what context do anxious clients explore their theological beliefs and values? As we have seen, organized religion carries less weight and authority than it used to, even for those who still embrace it as an important source of inspiration. For practitioners to take a hands-off approach toward a client's theology, ostensibly because it is something for the individual to explore with the clergy, demonstrates a profound lack of understanding of today's changing world. The therapeutic, as Philip Rieff (1987) has noted, has for better or worse supplanted, if not superseded, organized religion as the context for the formation and clarification of one's core beliefs and values. It has filled and continues to fill a significant void in American society and culture left by the decline of organized religion. Extending this thought, Frame (2003) writes,

> Because of the decline in religious practice in America during the past several decades, counselors and other mental health practitioners are serving as the culture's *shamans* when it comes to answering questions about the meaning and purpose of life and providing more direction for clients. It is possible, then, for counselors to think of themselves as partners with religion and spirituality striving toward common ends. (p. 18)

If we situate the void left by the decline of organized religion into the context of the new age of anxiety, then it really becomes something of a moral imperative for counselors and therapists to help guide their clients in the acquisition of new meaning. As I suggest in chapter 4, preparatory to helping anxious clients address questions of a theological and spiritual nature, practitioners must first be clear about their own theological beliefs and values and the extent to which they go about disclosing these to individuals in their care.

The suggestion that counselors and mental health practitioners use their personal theology as a resource in the counseling session is a departure from conventional psychotherapeutic paradigms. However, the traditional psychotherapeutic framework of having the therapist check his or her self at the door in the interest of therapeutic neutrality and objectivity stands in urgent need of reassessment, particularly in light of post–September 11 living. Moreover, the nature of supermodernity is such that clients are left breathless by the overt acceleration of history and by the overabundance of current national events and world affairs. In this context, if we as practitioners minimize our clients' meaning making, then we can expect their anxiety to increase rather than decrease. I argue that the intentional exploration of a client's theological beliefs and values is fundamentally in keeping with CBT, the treatment of choice for generalized anxiety as well as for the new anxiety. This presupposes a familiarity on the part of the caregiver with his or her own theological belief system and a willingness to be self-disclosive about those beliefs and values when called for in the counseling situation.

> The belief that therapists can and should keep their values out of therapy has been discredited because of penetrating critiques and accumulating empirical evidence to the contrary. . . . The belief that therapists could be value free was further undermined by the recognition of serious problems with traditional formulations of positivism. . . . Even so-called "objective" scientists have values that limit and bias their observations. . . . Psychotherapists have been forced to acknowledge that if basic scientific research cannot be value free, neither can an applied discipline such as psychotherapy. (Miller, 1999, pp. 135–136)

By now, some practitioners may be feeling anxious themselves about a therapeutic approach to anxiety that intentionally engages a client theologically, not to mention that it also encourages them to draw from their own theological frameworks in the counseling session. What about the role of appropriate boundaries? What about the danger of imposing one's religious beliefs and theological values on the client, someone who is in a more vulnerable and therefore less powerful position? What steps must the practitioner take to avoid any hint of "evangelizing" the client to his or her belief system? The questions are all legitimate and must be taken seriously. In chapter 5, I address these questions directly to develop more precise strategies that can assist practitioners in becoming careful participant observers of their theological interventions with anxious clients. In certain ways, what I put forward is a methodology for developing a rigorous hermeneutic of critique or suspicion applied to one's own theology and, maybe more important, to how we use our theology in the context of therapy and counseling. To be sure, venturing into the realm of theology as a way of helping anxious clients find new and reconstructed meaning in an age of change and transition requires great care, skill, and self-awareness. Without a hermeneutic of self-critique, practitioners are in danger of imposing their beliefs, values, and theology on unsuspecting clients. This is troubling enough with a client who is from the same or a similar faith tradition. It is even more troubling if practitioners proceed to impose their theological views on clients of a different faith tradition, as well as on those who describe themselves as nonbelievers. The solution, however, is not to avoid theology in counseling altogether, what psychotherapy has prescribed in years past. In an age of anxiety, clients need our help with the process of meaning making, something that practitioners, armed with a hermeneutic of self-critique, must be prepared to do.

For psychotherapists, mental health practitioners, and pastoral counselors, it is important to keep in mind that the world post–September 11 is very different from what it was before. There is always the nothing-new-under-the-sun argument—that is, anxiety is part and parcel of human life in every age—and there is certainly plenty of truth in this assessment. At the same time, the perception of many post–September 11 clients is that life has dramatically changed and not for the better. Along with the legitimate worries and concerns discussed earlier, there are countless other potential problems that fear entrepreneurs are determined to let us never forget. Practitioners, then, can rightly assume that some form of post–September 11 anxiety will be present to one extent or another with any given client. And to effectively treat today's anxious client, caregivers will need to develop comprehensive modalities of care that are inclusive of theological frames of reference. In other words, theology—both the client's and the practitioner's—must become integral to post–September 11 counseling and therapy. This presupposes the use of self on the part of the practitioner, including the appropriate application of his or her beliefs and values. As I point out in chapter 6, for some time now, the fields of psychotherapy, mental health counseling, and pastoral counseling have been espousing the use of the caregiver's self in the treatment process but only up to a point. The use of self, in the form of "being with" a client—or as Heinz Kohut (1984, as cited in Cooper-White, 2004) puts it, the conveying of empathic understanding and emotional responsiveness—has been a staple of the therapeutic process for years. Yet, in treating the new anxiety situated in the context of a supermodern post–September 11 world, more is required. To help unburden today's client of his or her anxiety, practitioners need to broaden their understanding of the use of self to include the intentional application of theological beliefs and values within the context of the counseling session. In so doing, we convey to our clients that it is indeed possible and even necessary to live meaningfully and purposefully in an age fraught with anxiety.

CHAPTER TWO

The Nature of Supermodernity

This is the precept by which I have lived. Prepare for the worst, expect the best, and take what comes.

—Hannah Arendt

The present age of anxiety is characterized by pressing concerns about the threat of terrorism, global warming, the beginning of the end of oil, immigration and pluralism, the widening economic gap between those who have and those who have not, and the outsourcing of American jobs. These concerns are legitimate, and they will demand our and our children's undivided attention for years to come. The anxiety that we feel is compounded daily or, in some cases, hourly by skilled fear entrepreneurs who know how to push our buttons. As if the issues listed here, eliciting legitimate concern and anxiety, were not enough, some fear entrepreneurs introduce a host of potentially threatening crises for our constant and ongoing consideration. We are bombarded in this information age by unrelenting news and images of real and fabricated crises that keep us constantly on edge. Thus, it becomes important to help those in our care find renewed hope and meaning, lest they succumb to the numbingly cynical fatalism espoused by those peddling fear.

Finding meaning in this age of anxiety, however, has its own unique set of challenges. Some attribute the difficulty to the collapse of meaning brought on by postmodernism. Indeed, postmodernists, for some time now, have been hard at work critiquing and deconstructing any and all systems of meaning, including and especially targeting those of a religious and theological nature.

Master stories or narratives are viewed with suspicion because, as postmodernist thinking goes, they are infused with no shortage of self-interest and personal power. The postmodernist theorist Jean Francois Lyotard defined postmodernism as "incredulity towards metanarratives," which we can take to mean the "dissolution of 'grand narratives' of belief and truth" (as quoted in Frosh, 2002, pp. 68–69, 96). This, in fact, is the heart of postmodernism: "the rejection of absolutes. Postmodernists usually insist that there can be no single rationality, no single morality, and no ruling theoretical framework for the analysis of social and political events." There are two other identifiable features along with the rejection of absolutes and grand narratives that help us understand more fundamentally the nature of postmodernism and its destabilizing impact on life in the Western world. The second feature, which I have already alluded to, "is the perceived saturation of all social and political discourses with power and dominance." We can add to this description, as postmodernists do, religious discourses and theological narratives of belief. Finally, a third feature of postmodernism concerns "the celebration of 'difference,'" the recognition and acceptance of a pluralistic world, and the relinquishment of the modern tendency to strive for sameness and uniformity (Kegan, 1998, pp. 324–326).

Where does this leave us as caregivers, working in an age of anxiety? Do we unhesitatingly embrace the first principle of postmodernism and work without any absolutes, without clear and compelling narratives of belief and meaning? In an age of anxiety, it is impossible and disadvantageous to clients for practitioners to avoid the process of meaning making in the context of counseling and therapy, even if the narratives by which we live are sprinkled with imperfections. Moreover, as the British psychoanalyst Stephen Frosh (2002) points out, "postmodernism, as an alternative response to the contradictions of modernism, is too intellectual and too incoherent (and too intellectually incoherent) for everyday practice" (p. 114). In the context of this study, we can say that postmodernism is too intellectual and incoherent for everyday therapeutic practice, particularly if we are working with anxious clients who are looking to us for help finding hope and meaning. This is not at all to discount the importance of the postmodern critique, which, with its deconstructive modus operandi, highlights quite effectively the infusion of personal interest and power into the formulation of any and all systems of meaning. That being said, if we want to be effective in our work with anxious clients, we need at our disposal not only a hermeneutics of critique and deconstruction but also one of reconstructed belief and meaning.

Reframing the Present Situation

The context in which we find the present age of anxiety is one that does not seem all that conducive to the formulation or reformulation of core narratives of belief and meaning. Viewed through a postmodernist lens, the situation reflects the collapse of meaning. Yet, is this—the collapse of meaning—really what we are talking about? It is, if and only if we are viewing the situation through a postmodernist lens. Viewed through another lens, however, say supermodernity, it is less about the collapse of meaning and more about the acceleration of meaning or, more fundamentally, the challenge of finding meaning in the overabundance of events that are literally here today and gone tomorrow. "We could say of supermodernity," writes the French anthropologist Marc Augé (1995),

> that it is the face of a coin whose obverse represents postmodernity: the positive of a negative. From the viewpoint of supermodernity, the difficulty of thinking about time stems from the overabundance of events in the contemporary world, not from the collapse of an idea of progress which—at least in the caricatured forms that make its dismissal so very easy—has been in a bad way for a long time. (p. 30)

Thus, in terms of helping clients find meaning in the present age of anxiety, practitioners would do well to bracket any postmodern assumptions about the collapse or demise of meaningful beliefs and values. The assumption conjures up negative images of a quasi wasteland lying in ruins, hardly a hopeful starting point for engaging the anxious client. Instead, if we begin from the standpoint of supermodernity, from the perspective of the acceleration of human life and history rather than from the collapse of meaning, we reframe the current situation more positively and therefore infuse our work with an element of legitimate hope.

Supermodernity, according to Augé (1995), is characterized by the overabundance of current events that are simultaneously ephemeral. This, in turn, leads to the real or perceived acceleration and impermanence of human life and history, which make our attempts at infusing the present with meaning more challenging and difficult. The acceleration and impermanence of life, however, are not only a reflection of the overabundance of information about national and world events. They also have to do with the context of life in the present, with what Augé describes as the appearance of the *nonplace*. He points out that

> if a place can be defined as relational, historical, and concerned with identity, then a space that cannot be defined as relational, or historical, or concerned

with identity is a nonplace. The hypothesis advanced here is that supermodernity produces nonplaces, meaning spaces that are not themselves anthropological places.

It is "a world thus surrendered to solitary individuality, to the fleeting, the temporary and ephemeral" and as such "offers the anthropologist (and others) a new object." In terms of "others," we can say, apropos to this particular study, practitioners treating the new anxiety. At a time when fear entrepreneurs attempt to exploit our anxiety over this crisis or that potential calamity, through a daily onslaught of facts, information, and news stories, it becomes imperative for all of us to have tangible places and communities to which we can turn to find authentic hope and meaning. But, in the context of supermodernity, characterized by an overabundance of nonplaces, finding hope and meaning requires a great deal of intentionality on the part of practitioners and those in their care. In fact, if caregivers are intent on engaging their clients at the level of belief and meaning, then the counseling or therapy session has the potential to become a thoroughly relational place concerned with the totality of one's identity. Thus,

> place and non-place are rather like opposed polarities: the first is never completely erased, the second never totally completed; they are like palimpsests on which the scrambled game of identity and relations is ceaselessly rewritten. But non-places are the real measure of our time; one that could be quantified—with the aid of a few conversions between area, volume and distance—by totaling all the air, rail, and motorway routes, the mobile cabins called "means of transport" (aircraft, trains and road vehicles), the airports and railway stations, hotel chains, leisure parks, large retail outlets, and finally the complex skein of cable and wireless networks that mobilize extraterrestrial space for the purposes of a communication so peculiar that it often puts the individual in contact only with another image of himself. (pp. 77–79)

Exchanging postmodernity for supermodernity, as a hermeneutical lens through which to observe and analyze the present age of anxiety, has the capacity to make us more hopeful as caregivers and therefore, as we part ways with certain postmodernists, less fatalistic. Contrary to postmodern interpretation, we are not talking about the collapse of meaning, let alone its disappearance. Rather, as viewed from the standpoint of supermodernity, the more fundamental issue lies in attempting to invest an overabundance of national and world events and crises with meaning before we are bombarded the very next day with a whole new set of events and crises. We cannot, in other words, keep up with the present pace of life unless we have a place where we can slow down, even for a moment, and reflect intentionally on what we believe about the particular issues germane to the events and crises. Practitioners, then, in working with today's anxious client, would do well to bracket any assumptions about postmodernism and the supposed collapse or disappearance of belief and meaning. What is most fundamentally exacerbating the new anxiety happens to be the overinvestment of meaning, the fact that human life and history have accelerated to such an extent that we have so little time to invest so many pivotal events with any kind of meaning. Augé (1995) writes,

> What is new is not that the world lacks meaning, or has little meaning, or less than it used to have; it is that we seem to feel an explicit and intense daily need to give it meaning: to give meaning to the world, not just some village or lineage. The need to give a meaning to the present, if not the past, is the price we pay for the overabundance of events corresponding to a situation we would call "supermodern" to express its essential quality: excess. (pp. 28–29)

Augé illustrates, rather vividly, the convergence of excess, overabundance, and acceleration with the new reality of nonplaces, by offering for our consideration a case study of sorts of a contemporary Frenchman. I choose to quote it at length because of its evocative power and the way that it captures, quite practically, the present reality of supermodernity. The parallels with American life, not to mention the rest of the Western world, are apparent:

> On the way to his car Pierre Dupont stopped at the cash dispenser to draw some money. The device accepted his card and told him he could have 1800 francs. Pierre Dupont pressed the button beside this figure on the screen. The device asked him to wait a moment and then delivered the sum requested, reminding him as it did so to withdraw his card. "Thank you for your custom," it added as Pierre Dupont arranged the banknotes in his wallet.
> It was a trouble-free drive, the trip to Paris on the A11 autoroute presenting no problems on a Sunday morning. There was no tailback at the junction where he joined it. He paid, at the Dourdan tollbooth using his blue card, skirted Paris on the *périphérique* and took the A1 to Roissy.
> He parked in row J of underground level 2, slid his parking ticket into his wallet and hurried to the Air France check-in desks. With some relief he deposited his suitcase (exactly 20 kilos) and handed his flight ticket to the hostess, asking if it would be possible to have a smoking seat next to the gangway. Silent and smiling, she assented with an inclination of her head, after first consulting her computer, and then gave him back his ticket along with a boarding pass. "Boarding from Satellite B at eighteen hundred," she told him.

He went early through Passport Control to do a little duty-free shopping. He bought a bottle of cognac (something French for his Asian clients) and a box of cigars (for himself). Meticulously, he put the receipt away next to his blue card.

He strolled past the window-displays of luxury goods, glancing briefly at their jewelry, clothing, and scent bottles, then called at the bookshop where he leafed through a couple of magazines before choosing an undemanding book: travel, adventure, spy fiction. Then he resumed his unhurried progress.

He was enjoying the feeling of freedom imparted by having got rid of his luggage and at the same time, more intimately, by the certainty that, now that he was "sorted out," his identity registered, his boarding pass in his pocket, he had nothing to do but wait for the sequence of events. "Roissy, just the two of us!": these days, surely, it was in these crowded places where thousands of individual itineraries converged for a moment, unaware of one another, that there survived something of the uncertain charm of the waste lands, the yards and building sites, the station platforms and waiting rooms where travelers break step, of all the chance meeting places where fugitive feelings occur of the possibility of continuing adventure, the feeling that all there is to do is to "see what happens."

The passengers boarded without problems. Those whose boarding passes bore the letter Z were requested to board last, and he observed with a certain amusement the muted, unnecessary jostling of the Xs and Ys around the door to the boarding gangway.

Waiting for take-off, while newspapers were being distributed, he glanced through the company's in-flight magazine and ran his finger along the imagined route of the journey: Heraklion, Larnaca, Beirut, Dhahran, Dubai, Bombay, Bangkok . . . more than nine thousand kilometers in the blink of an eye, and a few names which had cropped up in the news over the years. He cast his eye down the duty-free price list, noted that credit cards were accepted on intercontinental flights, and read with a certain smugness the advantages conferred by the "business class" in which he was traveling thanks to the intelligent generosity of his firm ("At Charles de Gaulle 2 and New York, Club lounges are provided where you can rest, make telephone calls, use a photocopier or Minitel. . . . Apart from a personal welcome and constant attentive service, the new Escape 2000 seat has been designed for extra width and has separately adjustable backrest and headrest . . ."). He examined briefly the digitally labeled control panel of his Escape 2000 seat and then, drifting back into the advertisements in the magazine, admired the aerodynamic lines of a few late-model roadsters and gazed at the pictures of some large hotels belonging to an international chain, somewhat pompously described as "the surroundings of civilization" (the Mammounia in Marrakesh, "once a palace, now the quintessence of five-star luxury," the Brussels Métropole, "where the splendors of the nineteenth century remain very much alive"). Then he came across an advertisement for a car with the same name as his seat, the Renault Espace: "One day, the need for space makes itself felt. . . . It comes to us without warning. And never goes away. The irresistible wish for a space of our own. A mobile space which can take us anywhere. A space where everything is to hand and nothing is lacking . . ." Just like the aircraft really. "Already space is inside you. . . . You've never been so firmly on the ground as you are in (the E)space," the advertisement ended pleasingly.

* * * *

They were taking off. He flicked rapidly through the rest of the magazine, giving a few seconds to a piece on "the hippopotamus—lord of the river" which began with an evocation of Africa as "cradle of legends" and "continent of magic and sorcery"; glancing at an article about Bologna ("You can be in love anywhere, but in Bologna you fall in love with the city"). A brightly coloured advertisement in English for a Japanese "videomovie" held his attention for a moment ("Vivid colors, vibrant sound and non-stop action. Make them yours forever"). A Trenet song, heard that afternoon over the car radio on the auto route, had been running through his head, and he mused that its line about the "photo, the old photo of my youth," would soon become meaningless to future generations. The colours of the present preserved forever: the camera as freezer. An advertisement for the Visa card managed to reassure him ("Accepted in Dubai and wherever you travel . . . Travel in full confidence with your Visa card").

He glanced distractedly through a few book reviews, pausing for a moment on the review of a work called *Euromarketing* which aroused his professional interest:

The homogenization of needs and consumption patterns is one of the overall trends characterizing the new international business environment. . . . Starting from an examination of the effects of the globalization phenomenon on European business, on the validity and content of Euromarketing and on predictable developments in the international marketing environment, numerous issues are discussed.

The review ended with an evocation of "the conditions suitable for the development of a mix that would be as standardized as possible" and "the architecture of a European communication."

Somewhat dreamily, Pierre Dupont put down his magazine. The "Fasten seat belt" notice had gone out. He adjusted his earphones, selecting Channel 5 and allowed himself to be invaded by the adagio of Joseph Haydn's Concerto No. 1 in E major. For a few hours (the time it would take to fly over the Mediterranean, the Arabian Sea and the Bay of Bengal), he would be alone at last. (pp. 1–6)

Notice the seeming warm feeling that comes over Pierre Dupont after getting himself situated in the Roissy Airport. In fact, it is as if, out of an unperceived feeling of loneliness and a longing for connection with someone or something, anything, he utters to himself, "Roissy, just the two of us!" There is, to be sure, a certain seductive quality to supermodernity: We feel as if we are genuinely connected to and rooted in particular places when in fact the places in which we find comfort, hope, and meaning are, in reality, nonplaces. It is similar to the feeling we get when we eat cotton candy at a summer fair or baseball game. Initially, the candy looks so good and inviting, as if it were comfort food. And then in a matter of minutes, it is gone and we wonder what we ate and why we ate it. But eat it we continue to do, as evidenced by the vendors who return again and again with a fresh supply. Similarly, nonplaces such as airports seductively give us the feeling that we are not alone and that we are connected; but this, of course, is nothing more than a fleeting illusion. As Augé (1995) suggests, in the world of supermodernity, it is in these crowded places—that is, nonplaces—that thousands of individual fragile identities converge just for a moment, oblivious to one another. We maintain, in other words, a connection with one another in the context of these "chance meeting places where fugitive feelings occur," drawn to the "possibility of continuing adventure." All we have to do is show up and "see what happens" without forming any meaningful and lasting connection with those around us. But, this comes at a rather steep price: perpetual alienation and disconnection precisely at a time in human history when we need to be meaningfully connected with one another.

The seductive nature of supermodernity—in particular, that of supermodern nonplaces—is that we are perpetually connected when, in reality, we are profoundly disconnected. It is, according to Augé (1995), a world that has surrendered to solitary individuality, to the fleeting, temporary, and ephemeral. And yet the illusion we embrace, if not live by, is that we are in a state of perpetual connection with one another, permanently tethered to this person and that person. Life is "meaningful" to the extent we show up to the chance meeting places, or nonplaces, to collectively see the parade of current events and the rapid acceleration of information directly before us. The reality, though, as Augé astutely notes, is that we are not connected at all or at least not meaningfully. As the theologian Paul Tillich (2000) pointed out some years ago, the feeling of alienation goes hand in hand with the feeling of anxiety. Only now, in the age of supermodernity, we are seduced into believing that we are perpetually connected—or, to use the current word, *wired*—when in reality we feel more isolated and more anxious than ever. Put another way, the supreme paradox of supermodernity is that at a time when we as a people are more connected and better wired than ever before, we are simultaneously more disconnected, alienated, and anxious. Our disconnectedness is reflected not only in the overabundance of information and current events, as well as the acceleration of human life and history, but even more so in the proliferation of nonplaces, which are inherently impersonal and impermanent. The painful irony is that in this present age of anxiety, the places where we seek connection, comfort, and even refuge are the very places that reinforce our feeling of solitary individuality. Furthermore, we are left with the sense that we are utterly on our own when it comes to getting our bearings and reorienting ourselves to a world that is very different from what it was even a few years ago.

The paradox of nonplaces is that we are surrounded by them, immersed in them, and yet they do little for us when it comes to assuaging our anxiety about the present and future state of the world. They are like the cotton candy, a temporary distraction that offers immediate gratification and a fleeting sense of connection—here this particular moment, gone and barely remembered the next. This we see with Pierre Dupont. It seems, at least initially, as if he has formed a meaningful connection with the Roissy Airport. However, immediately after boarding the aircraft, Dupont loses himself in the pages of the in-flight magazine, particularly, the pages of advertisements that offer him temporary escape into the world of other nonplaces: five-star luxury hotels, primitive parts of Africa, romantic Bologna, the world of duty-free goods, popular music, and so forth. His seeming connection to the airport ("Roissy, just the two of us!") is as fleeting and ephemeral as is his connection to the places—or, more precisely, the nonplaces—that he seems enamored with on the advertisement pages of the magazine. Augé (1995) therefore illustrates rather well how the accelerated pace of human life, the overabundance of information, the growing tangle of global interdependencies, and the tendency to seek comfort and connection in the context of nonplaces have the potential for heightening, rather than lessening, our feeling of apprehensiveness about the present and future. Because of the accelerated pace of living, which certainly characterizes supermodernity, there is simply not enough time to get our bearings let alone invest current events with any sort of substantive and lasting meaning. Even if we did have the luxury of more time for reflecting on the events of the day, the context for doing so at present, that is, nonplaces, is simply not conducive to the task of meaning making.

Augé (1995), as we have seen, provides us with several concrete examples of nonplaces, one of the defining features of supermodernity. In the case study, we see Dupont the businessman spending the day in the context of places that are extraordinarily common, ubiquitous, and impersonal: the ATM, an airport terminal, an aircraft, the advertisement pages of an in-flight magazine, and so on. The seat belt sign in Dupont's aircraft is turned off, letting passengers know that the aircraft is fully airborne. Dupont sits back and relaxes, turns on a Haydn concerto, and basks in the feeling that "he would be alone at last." At last? Augé has intentionally ended the case study on a note of profound irony, for Dupont has been alone throughout the entire day. The same is true for the rest of us who spend our days in the context of these nonplaces and other nonplaces listed by Augé: automobiles, railway stations, hotel chains, leisure parks, large retail outlets, and "the complex skein of cable and wireless networks" otherwise known as cyberspace—which could very well be the quintessential nonplace for this electronic day and age. Surfing the Internet, blogging, e-mailing, and instant messaging have fast become the primary means by which we get our news about the world, not to mention the way we attempt to stay meaningfully connected with one another. However, because of the disembodied nature of cyberspace, spending a significant portion of our lives "surfing the Web can be as much an experience of profound isolation and alienation as one of connection" (Cooper-White, 2004, p. 185).

It is important to note that in an age of anxiety, situated more fundamentally in the context of supermodernity, the challenge is to find a place where we can be guided in our attempts to make sense of a rapidly changing world. Yet, as we have discovered, the supermodern world makes this nearly impossible because of the proliferation of nonplaces. Like cotton candy, which gives us little more than temporary pleasure and satisfaction, nonplaces give us temporary comfort and meaning. We even seek a certain refuge in the nonplaces of the present, for they at least feel familiar and offer us a brief diversion from the complexities of supermodern life. We do our banking at the impersonal ATM where we do not have to see anyone or talk to anyone. We do our shopping at what Augé (1995) calls the "large retail outlets," otherwise known as the shopping mall, where, again, we do not have to talk to anyone unless, of course, we need to make a purchase. And even then, we do not have to say much of anything to the clerk at the cash register, nor does she or he have to say anything meaningful to us. It is a business transaction, pure and simple—as it is in the supermarket checkout line, only today we can avoid human interaction altogether by proceeding to the self-checkout to tally our own bill and settle accounts with a machine. Nor do we have to interact with the talking heads on the television; they inform us what we need to pay attention to in the world of current events, what we need to fear, and, for good measure, what it all means. We can sit back like passive spectators and easily let the purveyors of fear and alarm on the television do our meaning making for us. In cyberspace, there is the potential for more interaction, but, as I have noted, it is interaction characterized by considerable anonymity and disembodiedness.

Augé (1995) has French culture and society in mind as he describes the impact of supermodernity on the human individual. His assessment, however, is also applicable to Western culture in general and to American society in particular. The acceleration of human life, the overabundance of current events, the growing tangle of interdependences in the emerging global world system, and the centrality of nonplaces can all be seen in a recent *New York Times* editorial "Fries With That?" (2006):

> Sometimes it's all too easy to lose perspective in the modern world. . . . The *Times* reported that McDonald's has begun experimenting with a new way of routing menu orders at the drive-through window. The voice you hear at the squawk box comes not from an employee inside the restaurant but from a call center hundreds, if not thousands, of miles away. The order is then relayed to the front of the very restaurant where you are bodily present and filled as usual. A man who wants a Big 'n' Tasty in Wyoming and a woman who wants an Egg McMuffin in Honolulu may be placing their orders with the same teenager in California. Several customers, told of the fact, seemed taken aback.
>
> And yet, where is the surprise? There you sit, perhaps miles from home, idling in a car that was manufactured almost anywhere, burning gasoline refined from a substance pumped out of the ground who knows where and shipped, in all likelihood, across the ocean to be trucked to the station where you last filled up. Meanwhile you're talking to your best friend on your cell phone—and who knows how that works or where those signals go?—or listening to satellite radio beamed down from space. Yet what's really on your mind is the food they're getting together for you inside that McDonald's, made from cattle that once lived anywhere and potatoes that grew someplace else, all of it relayed from some way station in the McDonald's supply chain.
>
> Yes, a long-distance call center for a drive-through window is something to marvel at. The real wonder is that the call center isn't in Bangalore. (p. A-22)

A Necessary Place for Meaning Making

Life in America has reached such an accelerated pace that we are often left breathless and bewildered. Such is the state of existence in the context of supermodernity. But that is not all. The current state of breathless bewilderment just so happens to coincide with a new age of anxiety and its having to do with the pressing issues of terrorism, global warming, the urgent need for alternative fuel sources, immigration and pluralism, economic disparity, globalization, a growing sense of unpredictability when it comes to employment and retirement, and the outsourcing of American jobs. Life, as Augé (1995) points out, is moving at such an astonishing breakneck pace that we have little time to make sense of it. However, even if we did have the time for more in-depth reflection, it would not be a guarantee that we would put it to good use unless we locate a place for doing so in the midst of the proliferation of nonplaces. In the past, communities of faith have been the definitive place to which Americans have turned to make sense of anxious times. Now, more and more Americans are classifying themselves as *spiritual* or, more to the point, *spiritual but not religious*. Although there has been, as noted in the previous chapter, a significant decline in religious practice in America during the past several decades, there has been simultaneously a deep spiritual hunger on the part of many Americans. The problem is that contemporary spirituality is less and less anchored in any particular religious or theological tradition, and it has therefore become rather amorphous and free-floating, an undefined phenomenon. Moreover, *spiritual but not religious* connotes a solipsistic approach to meaning making that is removed from the relational, historical, and collective-identity dimensions of spiritual formation. The irony is that contemporary spirituality becomes something of another nonplace where we go to find temporary comfort and refuge. Because so many Americans are resistant to situating their spirituality in the context of religious faith communities, the place for spiritual development and meaning making becomes, almost by default, the counseling or therapy session. In the context of a therapeutic relationship built on trust and hope, the counselor or mental health practitioner becomes, to some extent, a *shaman*, or spiritual guide, ready to assist the client in reflecting on the meaning and purpose of life. By intentionally creating a space or place for spiritual exploration and meaning making, within the context of a culture increasingly characterized by the overabundance of nonplaces, the counselor or practitioner conveys that he or she is a partner with religion and spirituality in striving toward common ends (Frame, 2003).

What I am suggesting is that the inclusion of spiritual and theological beliefs and values in the work of psychotherapy, mental health counseling, and pastoral counseling is no longer optional in this new age of anxiety. Although it is true that formal, organized religious practice has been in steady decline for sometime, it is equally true that a deep spiritual hunger and quest to find new forms of meaning pervade American society and the lives of those in our care. But, again, contemporary spirituality, in its myriad individualistic forms, does not always have the capacity to sustain us, particularly at a time when there is no shortage of confusion and disorientation. It becomes yet another nonplace, an end in itself that gives us a fix of temporary relief from the travails of supermodern life. Without an overt connection to any core faith tradition, personal spirituality will have the potential of muddying the water of meaning making even further, at times doing more harm than good and exacerbating an individual's disorientation. Augé (1995) writes that "in Western societies, at least, the individual wants to be a world in himself; he intends to interpret the information delivered to him by himself and for himself." He adds,

> Sociologists of religion have revealed the singular character even of Catholic practice: practicing Catholics intend to practice in their own fashion. Similarly, the question of relations between the sexes can be settled only in the name of the undifferentiated value of the individual. Note, though, that this individualization of approaches seems less surprising when it is referred to the analyses outlined above: never before have individual histories been so explicitly affected by collective history, but never before, either, have the reference points for collective identification been so unstable. The individual production of meaning is thus more necessary than ever. (p. 37)

Individual meaning making, however, cannot occur in a solipsistic vacuum or nonplace. Rather, the individual production of meaning, more necessary than ever, requires the context of a relational place. In the past, the relational and historical place of choice for so many Americans was organized religion, where issues of ultimate meaning and collective and individual identity could be addressed intentionally and continually. But now, with the decline in religious practice, we are left with a void that makes meaning making a more challenging proposition. As Augé (1995) points out, even religious believers who remain connected to a particular faith tradition do so in a way that is individualistic and singular. In the language of supermodernity, the religious believer's spirituality is paradoxically something of another nonplace, even as it is situated in an organized faith tradition. Whether organized religion can transform itself and become, once again, the definitive place for meaning making remains to be seen. In the meantime, because of the relational nature of the work, therapy and counseling are poised to pick up the slack and fill some of the void left from the decline of religious practice. This does assume a willingness on the part of practitioners to think outside the box of conventional psychotherapeutic paradigms, which tend to leave discussions of ultimate meaning, including those having to do with God, to the priest or the minister. If organized religion were still the place where most Americans did their meaning making, then no problem, practitioners could leave religious beliefs and theological views to the religious professional while concentrating exclusively on matters of a psychological nature. But in an age characterized by the decline of organized religion, historically, the locus of meaning making, practitioners have a moral obligation to step into the void and intentionally help clients reflect on the meaning and purpose of their lives.

The point I am making is that therapy and counseling have a unique opportunity to offer more to clients than what they have ever offered before. In the context of a new age of anxiety, compounded by the reality of supermodernity, helping our clients with the task of finding meaning, purpose, and something to ground their lives in does not come a minute too soon. As we have seen, when many Americans feel particularly anxious about the present and future states of the nation and the world, they also feel as if they are on their own to make sense of the myriad dramatic changes that they read about in the newspaper or on the Internet or hear about nightly on cable news. The feeling of being on our own to find our way through this time of great change and transition is in keeping with the nature of supermodernity, which, as Augé (1995) suggests, subjects "the individual consciousness to entirely new experiences and ordeals of solitude, directly linked with the appearance and proliferation of non-places." Indeed, our preference for and dependency on nonplaces to give us at least a temporary feeling of comfort, refuge, and familiarity create, as it were, a "solitary contractuality." Augé writes,

> Alone, but one of many, the user of a non-place is in contractual relations with it (or with the powers that govern it). He is reminded, when necessary, that the contract exists. One element in this is the way the non-place is to be used: the ticket he has bought, the card he will have to show at the tollbooth, even the trolley he trundles round the supermarket, are all more or less clear signs of it. The contract always relates to the individual identity of the contracting party. (pp. 93, 94, 101)

The present age of anxiety, then, when we contextualize it as being situated not only in a post–September 11 world but even more so in the world of supermodernity, requires from practitioners new and creative approaches to care and counseling. Traditional psychotherapeutic paradigms and modalities, which emphasize therapeutic neutrality and the almost-obsessive concern with setting firm boundaries so as not to encourage overdependence and passivity with clients, now stand in need of immediate reassessment. America is and will be in a period of transition for some time to come, triggering feelings of anxiety in all of us. At the same time, because of the nature of supermodernity, there are fewer and fewer places that we can go to try to make sense of a world that leaves us confounded. For some Americans, organized faith communities are still the relational and historical place of meaning and memory. And yet, with more Americans identifying themselves as *spiritual but not religious*, the traditional locus of meaning making—that is, the church and synagogue—becomes less influential as a buffer against the new anxiety. This, again, is where mental health and psychotherapeutic and pastoral counseling practitioners must be willing to step in and fill the void left from the decline in religious practice. Moreover, viewed in the light of the rise and proliferation of nonplaces, practitioners have a moral obligation to create, in Winnicott's words (2005), a "holding environment" that is inclusive of the client's spiritual values and theological beliefs. In an age of anxiety exacerbated by "ordeals of solitude," the therapy session becomes the relational context in which the client's beliefs about the present and future are articulated, examined, strengthened, and/or revised and modified.

It is important to keep in mind that we are not simply talking about, as Augé (1995) points out, "a postmodern form of alienation" from the familiar grand narratives and traditions of the past. On the contrary, "the world of supermodernity does not exactly match the one in which we believe we live, for we live in a world that we have not yet learned to look at" (pp. 35, 118). The application of a supermodern lens suggests that the fundamental issue is not so much the loss or even the collapse of meaning, as postmodernism would have it. Rather, the core issue lies in trying to find meaning in the overabundance of daily events that are here today and gone tomorrow, having given way to a host of other events, information, and commentary by the following morning. But because of the ordeals of solitude lived out in the context of nonplaces, our attempts at making sense of the dramatic changes to our nation and world, of finding and making meaning, will be highly individualistic. We are, in many ways, on our own in terms of navigating the world that we have not yet learned or maybe even begun to learn to look at. Again, it is not simply the overabundance of world and national events that makes meaning making so difficult. The proliferation of nonplaces, which seductively offer us temporary relief and refuge from our worries and cares, makes finding a relational holding environment, where we can intentionally explore issues of belief, meaning, and purpose, even more challenging.

The new anxiety, then, has less to do with any collapse or lack of meaning and more to do with finding the requisite time and place needed for reorienting ourselves to the new world that we have not yet learned to look at. Nor will our fascination and preoccupation with nonplaces bring us any sense of lasting peace and comfort, for nonplaces, as we have seen, have to do with

> solitary individuality combined with non-human mediation (all it takes is a notice or a screen) between the individual and the public authority. . . . What is significant in the experience of non-place is its power of attraction, inversely proportional to territorial attraction, to the gravitational pull of place and tradition. This is obvious in different ways in the weekend and holiday stampedes along the motorways, the difficulty experienced by traffic controllers in coping with jammed air routes, the success of the latest forms of retail distribution.

There is simply too little time and not enough meaningful collective space for reorientating ourselves to the dizzying supermodern world. All of which, according to Augé (1995), comes at a rather steep price:

> A person entering the space of non-place is relieved of his usual determinants. He becomes no more than what he does or experiences in the role of passenger, customer, or driver. Perhaps he is still weighed down by the previous day's worries, the next day's concerns; but he is distanced from them temporarily by the environment of the moment. Subjected to a gentle form of possession, to which he surrenders himself with more or less talent or conviction, he tastes for a while—like anyone who is possessed—the passive joys of identity-loss, and the more active pleasure of role-playing. . . .
>
> What he is confronted with, finally, is an image of himself, but in truth it is a pretty strange image. The only face to be seen, the only voice to be heard, in the silent dialogue he holds with the landscape-text addressed to him along with others, are his own: the face and voice of a solitude made all the more baffling by the fact that it echoes millions of others. The passenger through non-places retrieves his identity only at Customs, at the tollbooth, at the check-out counter. Meanwhile, he obeys the same code as others, receives the same messages, responds to the same entreaties. The space of non-place creates neither singular identity nor relations; only solitude, and similitude. (pp. 103, 118)

Life in post–September 11 America is characterized by worries over the possibility of renewed terrorism, the destabilizing effect of global warming on climate and atmosphere, the depletion of oil and petroleum before we have viable alternative energy sources, the debate over assimilation versus maintaining one's original cultural identity in the context of the new wave of immigration, the reality of globalization and the outsourcing of American labor, the vanishing middle class, and so forth. There is no shortage of things to worry about, and certainly many if not all Americans are feeling anxious to one extent or another. It is, as Augé (1995) suggests, living in a world that we have not yet learned to look at, as if, like Rip Van Winkle, we awakened from a long slumber and are now confused and disoriented by the accelerated transformations of the contemporary world. There is clearly a great need to reorient ourselves to the changing world of the present, to find meaning in the here and now and thus resist the temptation "to look back from the upheavals of the present towards an illusory past stability" (p. 47). In a post–September 11 age of anxiety, life requires, in the words of Tillich (2000), the courage to be, which presupposes a dynamic and compelling system of belief and meaning. Waking up each day to a strange new world that we have not yet learned to look at, let alone make sense of, requires no shortage of courage from practitioners and those in their care. In addition, it requires a great deal of clarity from us about our own theological beliefs and spiritual values, how we find and make meaning in a post–September 11 world. A clearly thought-out and articulated method of finding theological meaning has important implications for our work with clients who are feeling disoriented and anxious. I have much more to say about this in chapter 4.

As I conclude this chapter, it is important to keep in mind that the new age of anxiety, situated in the broader context of supermodernity, is characterized by a considerable feeling of confusion and, even more so, disorientation. Augé (1995) is correct when he points out that because of the accelerated pace of life and the overabundance of information about national and world events, we are left in a kind of limbo, trying, as best we can, to acclimate ourselves to a world that we have only begun to look at. The situation necessitates, on the part of practitioners, a commitment to help clients reorient themselves to a world in transition by intentionally engaging them at the level of belief and meaning. We cannot, out of devotion to traditional paradigms of care—for example, therapeutic neutrality—sidestep the issue of belief and meaning in our therapy or counseling work or assume that these will be addressed elsewhere in some other context. With the decline in religious practice, combined with the proliferation of nonplaces, the therapy session may be the place most suitable for addressing, in depth, the client's core beliefs about the present and the future. If we rigidly cling to traditional paradigms of therapeutic neutrality, of leaving matters spiritual and theological to the religious professional, and of avoiding any disclosure of our own beliefs and values out of a fear that we may end up fostering overdependence or passivity, then we risk making our clients feel even more anxious and uncertain.

This applies to a traditional or classical psychoanalytic approach to therapy as well as to more contemporary forms of counseling, such as those put forward by self-psychology. For example, with self-psychology, there is certainly more openness to the use of self on the part of the therapist in the counseling session. This openness, however, has certain limitations. It is permissible for the therapist to use the fullness of self in the form of warmth, empathy, care, and the like. The use of self, in the form of disclosing or modeling beliefs and values about the present and future, is another matter altogether, something that would not be supported by some or, perhaps, many therapists. Still, the present age of anxiety, situated more broadly in the context of supermodernity, requires the capacity to think and work outside the box of traditional and even contemporary paradigms of care and counseling. This includes the willingness, on the part of the practitioner, to carefully and appropriately disclose his or her own beliefs and values in the counseling session, as a way of modeling for the client the courage to be. The client, in turn, will then have "permission" to disclose, explore, and clarify his or her own beliefs and values about life in the present world. This becomes, as it were, a pressure-release valve, as clients begin to feel less disoriented and more hopeful, the challenges of post–September 11 living notwithstanding. As practitioners, we do our work at present in a nation and world that are in transition, and along with our clients, we, too, struggle to get our bearings, to make sense of it all. It is as if we and those in our care are on a journey together through some strange land:

> The demands it makes on the powers of observation and description (the impossibility of seeing everything or saying everything), and the resulting feeling of "disorientation" . . . causes a break or discontinuity between the spectator-traveler and the space of the landscape he is contemplating or rushing through. This prevents him from perceiving it as a place, from being fully present in it. (Augé, 1995, pp. 84–85)

~

CHAPTER THREE

Diagnosing the New Anxiety

Life is not what it's supposed to be. It's what it is. The way you cope with it is what makes all the difference.

—Virginia Satir

Americans, as we saw in chapter 1, are on edge about the present and future state of the nation and world. Put more clinically, we are anxious about a world that we have not yet learned to look at, a world that in and of itself is in a state of tremendous change and transition. Moreover, that we have not yet even begun to get our bearings in this strange new post–September 11 world would suggest that making sense of it or finding some measure of meaning in it presents us with a significant challenge. How do we, for example, make sense of terrorist acts and threats of additional terrorism aimed at innocent Americans? True, there is nothing new under the sun when it comes to actual terrorism and threats of terrorism. Just ask any Israeli or Palestinian who has lived and continues to live with the reality of terror, 24–7. For Americans, however, living with the reality of terror on our own soil does symbolize a certain innocence or paradise lost, thus triggering to one extent or another in all of us apprehension and worry. But there is more: Can we even begin to comprehend what the world will be like, say, in our children's and their children's lifetime if the earth, as more and more scientists are predicting, continues to increase in temperature? What will happen when there is an increasingly shorter supply of oil at precisely the same moment that demand for it is greatest? Will there be turf wars, skirmishes, or, worse, all-out wars between nations vying for what is left of fossil fuels, desperately looking for ways to maintain economic and political stability? How will America traverse the so-called world or global system, particularly in light of the outsourcing of American labor, which just so happens to coincide with the disappearance of the middle class and the dangerously widening gap between those who have a piece of the American dream and those who do not? Abraham Lincoln, just before his election as president, stated emphatically, as he quoted from Jesus's Sermon on the Mount, that a house divided against itself cannot and will not stand. Furthermore, how does America remain united in the context of the new immigration as the minority-to-majority demographic becomes a reality and ethnic groups insist on retaining their original cultural identities?

As someone who teaches multicultural counseling, I am fully aware that mental health and well-being for culturally and ethnically diverse clients are correlative with the retention of one's original cultural identity (Sue & Sue, 2002). Yet, what will be the uniting factor that holds America together? How do we assimilate culturally diverse citizens into the fabric of American life? Can we even begin to determine what it will mean if ethnic or cultural groups resist the push toward assimilation? Europe, which is some years ahead of America with the multicultural experiment, offers us some clues:

> The multicultural fantasy in Europe . . . was that, in due course, assuming that the proper resources were committed and benevolence deployed, Islamic and other immigrants would eventually become liberals. As it's said, they would come to "accept" the values of their new countries. It was never clear how this vision was supposed to coexist with multiculturalism's other main assumption, which was that group identity should be maintained. But by now that question is largely academic: the European vision of multiculturalism, in all its simultaneous good will and self-congratulation, is no longer sustainable. And most Europeans know it. What they don't know is what to do next. (D. Rieff, 2005, pp. 11–12)

The issues listed here will not be resolved overnight or anytime soon, which means that we have entered a period of significant transition characterized by anxiety about the present and future direction of the nation and world. This, I argue, is the *new anxiety*, triggered by a profound sense of disorientation and a loss of bearings and familiar points of reference. The question is, how do we go about reorienting ourselves in the midst of the confusion and perplexity? Maybe even more fundamental is, where do we reorient ourselves? Where do we go to get our bearings, to restore our sense of balance? Where do we turn to find meaning, to explore, clarify, and fine-tune our spiritual values and theological beliefs? I remember that on the Sunday after September 11, 2001, the church I was attending in the San Francisco Bay Area was filled to capacity and overflowing as individuals, couples, and families flocked to a place that they believed would help them regain their bearings and make sense of the devastating events that had taken place earlier that week. And this happened all across the country, in community after community, as Americans entered houses of worship in droves those Sundays following the attacks of September 11. What we were seeking was, in the language of Augé (1995), a relational and historical place where we could reaffirm our collective identity, make some sense of the chaos and craziness, and come to terms with our anxiety and vulnerability. But with the decline in religious practice in American society combined with the fact that more Americans identify themselves as being spiritual but not religious, the extraordinary return of so many Americans to organized communities of religious faith in the days and weeks following September 11 was, not surprisingly, rather short-lived. Life returned to "normal," or at least we wanted to believe that it had or that it could.

Americans desperately wanted life to return to some semblance of normalcy and thus sought refuge in all the familiar places, which means in a supermodern world that we went back to looking for comfort and security in the context of nonplaces: the shopping mall, retail outlets, cyberspace, television, advertising, supermarket chains, the world of fast food, travel for no particular reason other than to get away, theme parks, hotel conglomerates, solipsistic forms of spirituality, and so forth. What we learned in the previous chapter, however, is that this flight into the seductive world of nonplaces does not alleviate our anxiety but exacerbates it. Nonplaces give us, if we apply the language of addiction, a temporary fix or escape, much like the addict experiences when he or she self-soothes with drugs or alcohol. But before too long, the pangs of pain, loneliness, and confusion return, even more powerfully than before, prompting us to seek out and use the drug all over again. In the same way, nonplaces are like a drug, giving us, at best, a rather temporary form of "release from the pain of uncertainty" (Frosh, 2002, p. 113). The operative word is *temporary*, illustrated by the proliferation and enormous popularity of nonplaces. On that Sunday and subsequent Sunday mornings back in September 2001, ministers encouraged their congregants to confess their vulnerability and confront the pain of uncertainty, which they did for a few weeks or months. But alas, time went by and the proverbial dust settled, and we sought once again release from the pain of uncertainty in the world of nonplaces. The new anxiety that had surfaced, that we had owned and acknowledged to ourselves and to one another, collectively in places of organized faith and worship, once again went underground where we would seemingly not have to deal with it. And yet, as Freud taught us so convincingly, the re-pressed can only stay repressed for so long, until that which is repressed resur-faces with renewed force, strength, and vigor. With the proliferation of fear entrepreneurs in public office, on the Internet, and, quintessentially, on nighttime cable television, it will never be long before the new anxiety re-turns or resurfaces with a vengeance.

Having situated the new anxiety into the context of post–September 11 and supermodern living, it is now time to inquire about the nature of the new anxiety itself. For example, what are the essential features of post–September 11 anxiety? Are they more or less consistent with the diagnostic criteria of anxiety as described in the *DSM–IV–TR*, or are they different? It is impor-tant for practitioners to be clear about this, lest they be treating one thing when in reality they are working with something else. In this chapter, I sys-tematically put forward the diagnostic criteria for the new anxiety. To sharpen the focus and as a point of comparison, I juxtapose the new anxiety with the diagnostic criteria for anxiety found in the *DSM–IV–TR*. Specifi-cally, the point of comparison is with GAD, which "first appeared as a diag-nostic category in the third edition of the *Diagnostic and Statistical Manual of Mental Disorders*" (Rygh & Sanderson, 2004, p. 1). As I note in chapter 1, the hallmark feature of GAD is excessive and uncontrollable worry. However, keep in mind the following question: Is this or is this not the case with the new anxiety? Moreover, as Capps (1999) has suggested, generalized anxiety is preemptive, felt in anticipation of real or imagined future events. In fact, he argues that anxiety is often disproportionate to actual environmental threats. This feature—the proportionality and disproportionality of anxiety toward real or imagined environmental threats and future events—is diag-nostic and particularly useful in distinguishing a more generalized form of anxiety from the new post–September 11 anxiety.

A Generalized Form of Anxiety

In 1844, the Danish philosopher Søren Kierkegaard (1981) took up the issue of anxiety in his famous work *The Concept of Anxiety* and in doing so estab-lished himself, as some believe, as the father of modern psychology. Kierkegaard made use of the word *angst*, which in German is alternately translated as *anxiety* or *fear*, whereas in Danish, Kierkegaard's native tongue, it is translated as *dread*. Anxiety, according to Kierkegaard, is deeply spiritual and existential, the price that we human beings pay for being consciously aware of our finitude and mortality. Kierkegaard put it this way:

No Grand Inquisitor has such dreadful torments in readiness as anxiety has, and no secret agent knows as cunningly as anxiety how to attack his suspect in his weakest moment or to make alluring the trap in which he will be caught, and no discerning judge knows how to interrogate and examine the accused as does anxiety, which never lets the accused escape, neither through amusement, nor by noise, nor during work, neither by day nor by night. (pp. 155–156)

In terms of the attack of anxiety by night, Kierkegaard was referring to the "2:00 A.M. dread" that overtakes us, that arouses us from a pleasant slumber and keeps us from falling back asleep. This dread, or anxiety, differs from fear in that fear is always related to a tangibly threatening object whereas the dread that awakes us in the middle of the night or preoccupies us during the day is an apprehensive anxiety that is felt in anticipation of real or imagined future events and a potentially threatening set of circumstances.

Kierkegaard has had a tremendous impact on the fields of philosophy and theology. For example, the influential work of the theologian Paul Tillich (2000) on modern anxiety reflects, to a certain extent, the work of Kierkegaard on angst and dread. Tillich set out in his classic work *The Courage to Be* to develop an ontology of anxiety, to describe its nature rather than the surface symptoms that the client presents in a counseling session. Tillich writes,

The first assertion about the nature of anxiety is this: Anxiety is the state in which a being is aware of its possible nonbeing. The same statement, in a shorter form, would read: anxiety is the existential awareness of nonbeing. "Existential" in this sentence means that it is not the abstract knowledge of nonbeing which produces anxiety but the awareness that nonbeing is a part of one's own being. It is not the realization of universal transitoriness, not even the experience of the death of others, but the impression of these events on the always latent awareness of our own having to die that produces anxiety. Anxiety is finitude, experienced as one's own finitude. This is the natural anxiety of man as man, and in some way of all living beings. It is the anxiety of nonbeing, the awareness of one's finitude as finitude. (pp. 35–36)

We can see that more than a century later Kierkegaard is still rather influential. Tillich, like Kierkegaard, develops an ontology of anxiety that is innately existential and spiritual. Anxiety, at bottom, has more to do with the modern human being's awareness that he or she is a finite creature situated in the world of universal transitoriness. Indeed, it is the modern human being who feels most acutely the truth put forward by Heraclitus of Ephesus: Nothing is permanent, except change and transitoriness. More recently, the

Swiss theologian Hans Urs von Balthasar (2000) has taken up the issue of anxiety, and he, too, like Tillich, is building on the work of Kierkegaard. Writing in *The Christian and Anxiety*, von Balthasar views anxiety as a fundamentally existential and spiritual phenomenon, exacerbated by the transitoriness and seeming meaninglessness of modern life:

> The particular case is the anxiety of modern man in a mechanized world where colossal machinery inexorably swallows up the frail human body and mind only to refashion it into a cog in the machinery—machinery that thus becomes as meaningless as it is all-consuming—the anxiety of man in a civilization that has destroyed all humane sense of proportion and that can no longer keep its own demons at bay. (pp. 35–36)

Von Balthasar, it should be noted, is linking modern anxiety with the collapse or the disappearance of meaning, as do the existentialists—theological, philosophical, and psychological—of last century. But the new post–September 11 anxiety of the supermodern world has less to do with the disappearance or collapse of meaning, as existentialists and postmodernists argue, and more to do with the difficulty of finding meaning in and attaching any meaning to the overabundant national and world events that are ever before us.

But that is not all. We can detect traces of Kierkegaard, more indirect but present nonetheless, in the pages of the *DSM–IV–TR* that describe the diagnostic features of GAD. For example, the *DSM–IV–TR* explains that "the essential feature of GAD is excessive anxiety and worry (apprehensive expectation), occurring more days than not for a period of at least 6 months, about a number of events or activities." This corresponds to Kierkegaard's apprehensive angst or dread that is felt in anticipation of real or imagined future events. Moreover, "the intensity, duration, or frequency of the anxiety or worry is far out of proportion to the actual likelihood or impact of the feared event" (pp. 423–433). According to Kierkegaard, fear is more emotionally proportionate because it has to do with a real and tangible threat or object, whereas anxiety is often out of proportion because the anticipated event or threat is merely perceived or imagined. The new anxiety, however, is more complex and therefore more difficult to diagnose in terms of its proportionality or disproportionality. The potentially threatening events—for example, further terrorism, the disappearance of coastlines due to global warming, the vanishing American middle class, and so forth—may not have come to pass as of yet; but if they do (and there is a fifty-fifty chance that they will), then life as we know it in this country will change dramatically. Thus, we might

reframe the discussion and ask, rhetorically, how can we not be feeling anxious with the potential threats ever before us, even if they do not occur today or even tomorrow? The anxiety may not be so disproportionate after all,
for if all or even some of these events do occur and we have not planned
ahead, then our children and our children's children will be facing a rather
uncertain future.

Traces of Kierkegaard can be found elsewhere in the *DSM–IV–TR*'s description of GAD. We read that

> the worries associated with Generalized Anxiety Disorder are difficult to con-
> trol and typically interfere significantly with functioning, whereas the worries
> of everyday life are perceived as more controllable and can be put off until
> later. Second, the worries associated with Generalized Anxiety Disorder are
> more pervasive, pronounced, distressing, and of longer duration and frequently
> occur without precipitants. . . . Third, everyday worries are much less likely to
> be accompanied by physical symptoms (e.g., excessive fatigue, restlessness,
> feeling keyed up or on edge, irritability). (p. 435)

Recall the language used by Kierkegaard to describe anxiety: the feeling of
angst or dread that awakens us with a start from a restful sleep, the subsequent restlessness and sleeplessness, the pervasive sense of worry and apprehensive expectation that takes much of the joy out of living, and so on. Anxiety, particularly that which is pathological, is as Kierkegaard described so
powerfully, like a Grand Inquisitor who tracks us down and never lets us escape, not through amusement, nor by noise, nor during work, neither by day
nor by night. If we situate this into the context of a supermodern world, we
can say, echoing Kierkegaard, that the new anxiety never lets us escape, not
through the amusement of nonplaces, such as the Internet or the world of instant messaging or the shopping mall; not by the noise of the television, the
cell phone, or the jet airliner; neither by day nor by night. Even today, with
all of the distractions, the Grand Inquisitor of anxiety will relentlessly track
us down and not let us escape.

At this point, it would be helpful to have a more comprehensive knowledge of GAD, before attempting to formulate the diagnostic criteria for the
new anxiety. The *DSM–IV–TR* systematically lists the diagnostic criteria for
GAD as such, with the first point composing the essential feature:

> A. Excessive anxiety and worry (apprehensive expectation), occurring more
> days than not for at least 6 months, about a number of events or activities
> (such as work or school performance).
> B. The person finds it difficult to control the worry.

C. The anxiety and worry are associated with three (or more) of the following six symptoms (with at least some symptoms present for more days than not for the past 6 months). Note: Only one item is required in children.
(1) restlessness or feeling keyed up or on edge
(2) being easily fatigued
(3) difficulty concentrating or mind going blank
(4) irritability
(5) muscle tension
(6) sleep disturbance (difficulty falling or staying asleep, or restless unsatisfying sleep)
D. The focus of the anxiety is not confined to features of an Axis I disorder, e.g., the anxiety or worry is not about having a Panic Attack (as in Panic Disorder), being embarrassed in public (as in Social Phobia), being contaminated (as in Obsessive-Compulsive Disorder), being away from home or close relatives (as in Separation Anxiety Disorder), gaining weight (as in Anorexia Nervosa), having multiple physical complaints (as in Somatization Disorder), or having a serious illness (as in Hypochondriasis), and the anxiety and worry do not occur exclusively during Posttraumatic Stress Disorder.
E. The anxiety, worry, or physical symptoms cause clinically significant distress or impairment in social, occupational, or other important areas of functioning.
F. The disturbance is not due to the direct physiological effects of a substance (e.g., a drug of abuse, a medication) or a general medical condition (e.g., hyperthyroidism) and does not occur exclusively during a Mood Disorder, a Psychotic Disorder, or a Pervasive Developmental Disorder. (pp. 435–436)

What is not stated in the synopsis of the diagnostic criteria for GAD is the importance of proportionality and disproportionality in the clinical assessment. It does, however, appear in the narrative portion of the *DSM–IV–TR*'s description of GAD: "The intensity, duration, or frequency of the anxiety and worry is far out of proportion to the actual likelihood or impact of the feared event." Assessing the proportionality of anxiety to a perceived threat or future event is, of course, a tricky undertaking, mostly because it is an imprecise science. In other words, a certain degree of subjectivity enters the picture anytime a practitioner is called on to assess the proportionality of anxiety to an actual, perceived, or imagined set of circumstances on the part of a particular client. Other subjective factors that influence a clinical assessment of anxiety include the practitioner's comfort level with ambiguity, the degree to which he or she views anxiety as part and parcel of human living or simply as a pathology that must be eradicated at all costs, the capacity to tolerate human suffering, the threshold of emotional and psychological pain and discomfort, and so forth. All of this, to be sure, affects either directly or in-

directly the practitioner's clinical assessment of the proportionality of generalized anxiety. That being said, the *DSM–IV–TR* gives us an important diagnostic framework for treating the anxious client. There is, as I have been noting, the proportionality or disproportionality factor, in which the intensity,
duration, or frequency of the client's anxiety does not match the particular
set of circumstances, actual or anticipated. In addition,

> the person finds it difficult to keep worrisome thoughts from interfering with
> attention to tasks at hand and has difficulty stopping the worry. Adults with
> Generalized Anxiety Disorder often worry about everyday, routine life circum-
> stances such as possible job responsibilities, finances, the health of family
> members, misfortune to their children, or minor matters (such as household
> chores, car repairs, or being late for appointments). (p. 433)

How we go about determining the proportionality of a client's anxiety,
worry, or apprehensive expectation can be illustrated with case material from
my own clinical practice of pastoral counseling and mental health counseling. David was a recent graduate with an MBA from a prestigious university.
He had aggressively circulated his resume to dozens and dozens of potential
employers but had yet to receive a firm job offer. In terms of birth order,
David is a firstborn, which meant that as the elder son of Irish American parents, he had great expectations placed on him to achieve and be successful.
A highly motivated young man in his midtwenties, he was, as we might expect, more than a little anxious. When David first came to see me, his presenting issue was "I'm a little concerned about my future." David, as I would
soon see, was minimizing his concern about the future, for it became readily
apparent that he was a great deal concerned about the future, especially
when he would receive another rejection letter from a business or company
and when a former classmate would call to share the good news that he or
she had secured employment. I diagnosed David with GAD; he was, after all,
presenting the hallmark feature of excessive worry and apprehensive expectation disproportionate to the given set of circumstances. Though not meaning to downplay David's sense of disappointment and frustration, I thought it
was clear that he was "catastrophizing" about the future, hastily jumping to
all kinds of fatalistic conclusions. Along with presenting the hallmark feature
of excessive worry, combined with demonstrating the difficulty of keeping it
under control, David was presenting more than three of the symptoms listed
in Criterion C: He was noticeably restless and on edge during the counseling
and, as he reported, was "always keyed up outside of our sessions"; he was fatigued, mostly attributable to erratic sleep patterns; and he found himself

getting increasingly irritable with his parents, his girlfriend, the classmates who would call him, and even strangers he would pass by on the street. Furthermore, at the odd jobs he was working out of necessity to pay the bills, he could not stay focused, largely because the work was not stimulating. The following is a pivotal vignette that illustrates the applicability of the GAD diagnosis to David:

> DAVID: I can't stay focused.
>
> KB: On what?
>
> DAVID: On anything!
>
> KB: For example?
>
> DAVID: You know, work. It's not what I prepared for. I have an MBA from a good school, and I'm stuck working as a financial advisor to families at a local bank. "Should we put our money in a CD? In bonds? In a money market? In a mutual fund?" That's what I deal with every day.
>
> KB: You sound frustrated.
>
> DAVID: I thought by now I'd have landed at the very least an entry-level management position with a prestigious company. All that hard work for nothing. And I still have loans to pay back. I'll be in debt forever with the salary I make. I can't sleep at night thinking about it.
>
> KB: Don't you think you're jumping to conclusions just a bit? After all, you're 25, just getting started in the world of finance, with a lot of working life ahead of you.
>
> DAVID: That makes sense, but so much is riding on me getting a good job and salary.
>
> KB: For whom?
>
> DAVID: For me. And for my parents. You don't know what it's like to live with that kind of pressure to succeed.
>
> KB: Help me understand.
>
> DAVID: For as long as I can remember, it's been "Let me see your report card. How are your grades? If you don't apply yourself and get a good job, you're not going to make it in today's world."
>
> KB: Sounds like you've internalized those messages rather powerfully.
>
> DAVID: I just don't want to disappoint my parents. They sacrificed so much to put me through school. I don't want to disappoint Erica [*David's girlfriend*] either. I know she wants to be with a successful guy. Sometimes I feel judged when I'm with her. She never puts me down directly. It's a feeling I get.
>
> KB: David, it does sound as if you're under a lot of pressure. I wonder how you're holding up?
>
> DAVID: Not very well. I pray about it every day . . . that God will give me some relief from all the pressure.
>
> KB: And what would that look like?

DAVID: A good job, getting married, having a family. I thought by now I'd at least have the first two. What keeps me awake at night is thinking this is as good as it's going to get. I'll always be working in some mediocre job, in debt, no wife, no kids.

KB: Sounds pretty bleak. What if we reframed all of this as a temporary situation, as something you have to cope with for the time being rather than for the rest of your life?

DAVID: I know what you're saying. But it's so hard to control it.

KB: Control what?

DAVID: The worry. I went to Erica's church on Sunday, and the minister told us that Jesus says we're not supposed to worry. And that makes me worry.

KB: About what?

DAVID: That I'm letting God down. I try to believe and have faith about the future, but it's so difficult. I can't turn off the worry, and yet I know that if you want to be a spiritual person, you can't worry about the future. That's what Erica's minister said on Sunday . . . more or less.

KB: Almost sounds like a double whammy.

DAVID: What do you mean?

KB: You're feeling anxious about the present and future, and on top of that, you're feeling anxious about feeling anxious. That's what I mean by a "double whammy."

DAVID: I just can't seem to turn it off.

KB: What if we simply deal with one of these at a time, starting with the worry itself apart from the value judgments about whether it's right or wrong, good or bad, or pleasing or not pleasing in the eyes of God? How does that sound?

DAVID: I know. It's just that the worry gets stronger, and I lose control and can't help myself.

David, as we can clearly see from the case vignette, presents with the hallmark feature of GAD (excessive and uncontrollable worry about future events and circumstances) and its accompanying symptoms (restlessness or feeling on edge, fatigue because of sleep disturbance, difficulty concentrating or focusing, and irritability). Although he does have legitimate concerns about satisfaction with his job and career, the debt accumulated from school loans, and the future of the relationship with his girlfriend, the intensity, duration, and frequency of his anxiety and worry are certainly far out of proportion to the actual likelihood or impact of the feared events. David may very well feel frustrated at not getting the management position that he had dreamed of and at having to work a job that is not particularly stimulating to him, but—and this is important—it does not mean that he will be working this job as a financial advisor at a local bank for the rest of his working life or that he will never work in management at a more prestigious financial firm. He may very well feel frustrated with the turn of events that leave him saddled with sizable debt from school loans and a current salary that precludes paying any more than the minimum monthly payment, but this does not mean that he will always have the salary or the student loan debt that he now has. And there may very well be a sense of ambiguity with his relationship with Erica, but again, this does not mean that he will never marry or have a family. David, as pointed out earlier, has a tendency to catastrophize about the future, to jump to fatalistic conclusions about possible future events that could happen but in all likelihood probably will not take place. He, then, is a textbook case illustrating GAD and the hallmark feature of uncontrollable worry disproportionate to a given set of circumstances that very likely will not occur.

Jim, however, is anxious about the future, too, but would not be diagnosed with GAD, because the intensity, duration, and frequency of his anxiety are more proportionate to the impact of future events should they occur. A 49-year-old father of three children, Jim is a computer programmer in Silicon Valley who rode the dot-com wave to financial success during the 1990s. Initially employed by a rather high-profile computer company, he, like so many others at the time, felt the urge to venture out on his own and start a brand-new dot-com company. At the time, the going was particularly good, and there was a great deal of money to be had, another California gold rush of sorts. But with the first gold rush, the money went to a few, whereas others lost everything. A century and a half later, the same thing happened, this time not in the hills of California but outside of San Jose. Jim, like so many other dot-comers of the late-1990s, never could foresee what lay ahead of him in a few short years: the bursting of the dot-com bubble, which would leave so many white-collar professionals out of work and out of money. For Jim, it was both: His new dot-com business went under, and he lost everything, save for the house that he and his family lived in. However, because he was out of money and had no income (he was told in no uncertain terms by his former employer that, because of downsizing, he should not expect to get his job back in the future), he was forced to use the money from his retirement fund to cover the mortgage, property taxes, home repairs, monthly utilities and expenses, and so forth. Jim is now the sole breadwinner in the family because his wife, a former school teacher, can no longer work. She was diagnosed with multiple sclerosis shortly before the collapse of Jim's dot-com business, adding to the stress and anxiety level of the family. The two oldest children, a boy and girl, both middle schoolers, have had to adjust to going without new clothes, sporting equipment, and electronic gadgetry that "all" their other friends have. Jim's youngest son, a fifth grader, was recently diagnosed with dyslexia, prompting the doctor to strongly encourage Jim to consider private and alternative forms of education. Jim, as we might expect, was suffering from worry and apprehensive expectation about his and his family's future. The worry, not surprisingly, occupies a great deal of his thinking during the day and keeps him awake during the night. He reports that he is always tired and is in need of a massage to help his body relax:

JIM: I feel like I'm in a vice grip that keeps getting tighter and tighter.

KB: You're under a lot of pressure, Jim. How are you holding up?

JIM: Good question. Some days better than other days.

KB: How about today? Right now?

JIM: I just feel overwhelmed. If only I had . . .

KB: Only had what?

JIM: Not taken such a huge financial risk. Actually, I'd still be out of work from the downsizing of the other company. But I'd not have used up all of my savings, and I'd have gotten a substantial severance package. What the hell was I thinking? I've managed to totally screw up the future for my family.

KB: What's the most pressing concern for you today?

JIM: Finding employment. Getting a paycheck. Getting benefits. I've used up all my savings, and now I'm using up all my retirement money. I need income soon, or we'll have to sell the house. The co-pay for my wife's medical expenses isn't cheap. And now I have to think about sending my son to a private school.

KB: You do sound overwhelmed. You mentioned last time that you had found some work. How is that going?

JIM: Sporadic. A couple consulting jobs, but they've come and gone. So has the money I made. A friend has a painting business, and I'm going to do some work for him. I've sent out dozens of resumes but nothing. The rejection gets old. I'm either too old or too overqualified or whatever. Pretty sad, isn't it?

KB: Sad? Meaning?

JIM: Pathetic! I've let my family down, and it's going to take a long time to work my way out of this hole . . . if ever.

KB: Can I go back to my earlier question: How are you holding up under all this pressure?

JIM: I don't know [*tears fill his eyes*]. I'm glad I can come here every week. I can't talk about this with my wife. She has her own problems. I've talked to my minister a couple of times, but his advice is too trite for me: "Trust God! Believe! Pray! Have faith!" And the one that gets me the most: "All things work together for good!" Give me a break!

KB: Religious platitudes can really push our buttons. Sounds like the minister, trying to be helpful, does more harm than good.

JIM: I just don't get it. I take my family to church every Sunday, try to live a moral life devoted to God, and look at my life. It doesn't add up.

KB: How are you holding up?

JIM: You know . . . I can't sleep at night because my mind is racing: What happens when I use up my retirement fund? How do I cover my wife's medical bills? What will I and the kids do when she loses her speech and bodily functions? I just feel exhausted. I can't turn it off during the day either. I'm doing a job around the house, and without even being aware of it, I get distracted. Ten or fifteen minutes go by, I've wracked my brain thinking of every possible scenario to get out of this damn predicament, and the job's still sitting there waiting to get done.

How do we diagnose Jim? Is he, like David, suffering from GAD? He certainly presents with the hallmark feature of the disorder, namely, excessive worry and apprehensive expectation about the future. In addition, he presents enough of the accompanying symptoms to be a candidate for GAD: He is in fact keyed up or on edge; he is frequently fatigued, if not exhausted; he is prone to distraction and to losing his focus; he requires a periodic massage to reduce the tension in his muscles; and his sleep patterns are highly erratic and unpredictable. Jim, like David, could be diagnosed with GAD if it were not for the fact that given his particular set of circumstances, the intensity, duration, and frequency of his anxiety and worry are not that disproportionate to the impact of certain events should they occur. And occur they might if he does not soon secure steady employment with the requisite income for living in one of the most expensive parts of the country. If Jim does not find steady employment soon, with the income and benefits needed to sustain a family living in Silicon Valley, he will need to sell the house or, because he has already missed several monthly mortgage payments, face a foreclosure action by the bank. Moreover, if he does not find steady employment with a substantive income soon—and the prospects are not looking promising—he will not be able to afford the private education that a child with severe dyslexia requires. Nor will he be able to cover the medical expenses for his wife. And whether he does or does not find employment, the burden of financial and emotional responsibility for the family will be increasingly his and his alone as his wife's health deteriorates. Furthermore, the future appears as if it will entail Jim's having to "disappoint" his other two children by not being able to afford new clothes for them, not having the money to take them on ski trips to Lake Tahoe, and not having the financial resources to provide them with, in their words, "the things all our friends have." Again, Jim presents with the essential features and accompanying symptoms of

GAD, yet the anxiety that he is experiencing is not disproportionate to the impact of feared events that are looming on the not-too-distant horizon. If circumstances in Jim's life do not change for the better sometime soon, then he faces a particularly difficult and uncertain future for himself and his family. I return to this theme—the proportionality and disproportionality of anxiety—in the context of discussing the new anxiety.

CBT: The Treatment of Choice

Before turning to this theme, it is important to address the treatment of generalized anxiety to glean important clues for how best to go about treating the new anxiety. Barlow (2002), one of the foremost authorities on the treatment of generalized anxiety, helps us preparatory to treating it to sharpen our understanding of its nature as compared with those of other mental disorders. Barlow points out that an essential distinguishing feature between anxiety and, for example, depression is that "depression tends to remit whether treated or not, usually in a matter of months" whereas anxiety tends to be "chronic and to remain present in somewhat less severe forms even if successfully treated" (p. 19). Given the chronic nature and, in certain cases, intractability of anxious apprehension and expectation, it is important for practitioners to approach the treatment of anxiety with a great deal of patience and empathic understanding, even toward a client like David whose worry is disproportionate to the likely occurrence of feared future events. To be sure, David and, for that matter, Jim, want desperately to feel more in control of their lives and less at the mercy of fate and happenstance. Barlow is convinced that "anxious apprehension is primarily characterized by a sense of an inability to predict or control future events that are personally salient." Barlow's theory is laid out in more detail in Rygh and Sanderson's *Treating Generalized Anxiety Disorder* (2004):

> [Anxious apprehension] is described as a state of high negative affect that is part of a diffuse cognitive-affective structure. Chronic tendencies of sensing events as unpredictable and/or uncontrollable presumably result from a developmental history in which opportunities to predict or control both aversive (e.g., punishment) and appetitive (e.g., attention, food, etc.) stimuli were insufficient. Parenting styles of noncontingent and/or negatively contingent (via overprotective, intrusive, or punitive) responses to a child's attempts to control vital events in the environment presumably produced a cognitive template of an external locus of control within that child. Barlow considers an external locus of control a major psychological vulnerability factor for the development

of anxiety disorders. Barlow posits that anxious apprehension is a state of help-lessness caused by the perception that one is unable to predict, control, or ob-tain vital results, with a strong physiological substrate of arousal or readiness for counteracting this state of helplessness. . . . According to Barlow, an anxi-ety disorder can be said to exist only if there is anxious apprehension over the possibility of experiencing an alarm response or any other type of negative event in the future. The negative affect associated with the sense of unpre-dictability and/or uncontrollability can be evoked by a variety of external and internal cues. Once evoked, anxious apprehension is a response that relies heavily on various cognitive processes. The cues that evoke anxious appre-hension presumably tap the cognitive-affective structure of associated stimu-lus, response, and/or meaning propositions stored in long-term memory. (p. 13)

If, in fact, anxious apprehension does tap the cognitive-affective structure of associated stimulus, response, and meaning propositions stored in long-term memory, then it is important for practitioners to carefully consider their meth-ods of treatment. For example, although psychodynamic modalities may prove helpful in treating certain issues and disorders, their effectiveness with the treatment of generalized anxiety is not as reliable. Encouraging David or Jim to undergo an analysis of several years may bring to light repressed issues and feelings, but there is no guarantee that even after several years of psychoana-lytic treatment, the cognitive-affective structure of associated stimulus, re-sponse, and meaning propositions will be fundamentally altered. Nor will the exploration of archetypal images and patterns, though not unimportant in other psychotherapeutic settings, bring about fundamental change to the cog-nitive-affective structure triggered in stressful moments of crisis and change. What, then, is the alternative? If psychodynamic modalities of treatment—for example, psychoanalysis and its derivatives, Jungian analysis, and so on—are not as effective in altering the cognitive-affective structure underlying anxious apprehension and expectation, then what is? "To date, the only psychosocial treatment with proven efficacy is cognitive–behavioral therapy," making it, or so we would think, the treatment of choice for practi-tioners in their work with anxious clients. And yet "despite the fact that CBT is the only psychosocial treatment meeting criteria as an empirically sup-ported treatment for GAD . . . it appears as though only a minority of such pa-tients receive this intervention" (Rygh & Sanderson, 2004, pp. 194–195).

In terms of generalized anxiety and the new post–September 11 anxiety, the central cognitive component "consists of perceptions of threat, as well as cognitive responses to these threat perceptions. Cognitive activity is appar-ent in images, thoughts, assumptions, and/or beliefs" (Rygh & Sanderson, 2004, p. 19). Note that when we begin to develop a systematic diagnosis for the new anxiety, the images, thoughts, assumptions, and, especially, beliefs will factor greatly in one's clinical and professional assessment of an anxious client. In the context of supermodernity, where clients struggle to make sense of a world characterized by the overabundance of events, the acceleration of time, the proliferation of nonplaces, and excessive fear mongering, what clients think and believe about the present and the future will significantly determine the extent to which they are feeling anxious. Put another way, in a supermodern post–September 11 world characterized by tremendous change and transition, one's capacity to make and remake meaning and to clarify and reclarify certain beliefs about the present and the future will determine the degree to which worry can be managed and held in check. What CBT can do for generalized anxiety it can also do for the new post–September 11 anxiety. For now, it is important to note that

> GAD can be modulated with a wide variety of techniques. These techniques include psychoeducational, cognitive restructuring (CR), hypothesis testing, positive imagery, worry exposure, improving problem orientation, cost-benefit analysis of coping, and two cognitive response prevention techniques: scheduled worry time and worry-free zones. (Rygh & Sanderson, 2004, p. 21)

It is not too difficult to see that the list of CBT techniques for the treatment of anxiety can be and needs to be inclusive of interventions having to do with meaning making and the clarification of beliefs and values.

The essence of CBT is its focus on the thinking of the client: "Emotions, behavior, and the environment are all considered important, but the distinguishing feature of cognitive therapy is its concentration on the client's beliefs, attitudes, and cognitions" (McMullin, 2000, p. 7). This can very well explain the reluctance on the part of so many practitioners to apply CBT to the treatment of anxiety despite its being "the best available empirically based psychotherapeutic intervention for GAD at this time" (Rygh & Sanderson, 2004, p. 194). Indeed, many practitioners trained in the context of psychodynamic or depth-oriented therapy, with the emphasis being primarily placed on feelings and emotions and guiding the client toward emotional awareness and catharsis, may find it difficult to accept that the mere reconfiguration of thoughts and beliefs can fundamentally alter cognitive-affective structures. Studies from the mid- to late 1990s demonstrate that only one in three clients reported receiving CBT forms of treatment. What researchers discovered was that

> dynamic psychotherapy was still the most frequently used therapeutic approach. A particularly surprising finding was that the percentage of patients

receiving cognitive or behavioral treatments had actually decreased from the percentage in a survey conducted . . . 5 years earlier. . . . One would expect an increase—not a decrease—in the use of evidence-based treatments, with the growing body of research and emphasis on evidence-based practice in recent years.

The implication for all psychotherapists, mental health practitioners, and pastoral counselors is that whether we are treating GAD or any number of other mental disorders,

> the increasing penetration of managed care, and the development and proliferation of clinical practice guidelines and treatment consensus statements, have raised the stakes for accountability. The failure to train practitioners in evidence-based treatments may lead to the fall of psychotherapy as a first-line effective treatment, despite considerable data supporting its efficacy. (p. 195)

As noted, CBT, the best available empirically based therapeutic intervention for the treatment of anxiety, focuses primarily on the thought patterns of clients. This, again, will require many practitioners to think outside the box of traditional paradigms and therapeutic modalities, if they have not already begun to do so. True, many of us would not be considered pure "disciples" of one particular school of psychological thinking, as was so often the case in the early years of the past century. Though most practitioners today would describe themselves as "eclectic," dynamic or depth-oriented paradigms and modalities still wield tremendous influence over psychotherapeutic practice. The need for clients, especially those who are anxious, to reflect on their thoughts, beliefs, and spiritual and theological values could, if practitioners are not careful, take a backseat to more familiar psychodynamic interventions: focusing on feelings and emotions, encouraging the full expression of feelings and emotions that will ideally lead to emotional catharsis, and, finally, helping clients work through their assorted and painful feelings and emotions. All well and good except for the fact that when it comes to the treatment of anxiety, depth-oriented psychotherapy, from an empirical standpoint, is not the most efficacious form of treatment. Psychodynamic treatment certainly has its time and place, such as in the area of unresolved grief. With generalized anxiety, however, and with the new post–September 11 anxiety, CBT and its variety of therapeutic techniques undoubtedly compose the most efficacious form of clinical treatment and intervention.

It has been demonstrated by way of empirical research that CBT is the treatment of choice with anxious clients. And CBT, unlike more traditional forms of psychodynamic therapy that focus on feelings and emotions, emphasizes the importance of thoughts. Feelings, emotions, and the environment are still worthy of consideration, but the feature that distinguishes cognitive therapy from other psychotherapeutic modalities is the primary focus on the client's beliefs, assumptions, and cognitions. McMullin (2000), writing in *The New Handbook of Cognitive Therapy Techniques*, argues that

> the first step in any cognitive therapy is to teach clients the importance of thoughts. Therapists must show clients that beliefs, philosophies, and schemata can cause powerful emotions and behaviors, and that to reduce or eliminate negative emotions, clients must change their beliefs. This is not a casual process; therapists need to use a systemic method to explain these principals.

He continues,

> Before clients can employ cognitive techniques effectively, they must be convinced that their beliefs are connected to their problems. Initially, most clients don't think so. They may blame genetics, parental mistreatment, traumatic childhood experiences, bad luck, hostile intent of others, an ill-formed society, or an insensitive, incompetent government. They accuse everybody and everything—except their own cognitive processing—for their emotional pain.
>
> The reason for their omission is evident. Their thoughts occur so rapidly and seem so ethereal that many clients don't notice that they are thinking anything at all. All they perceive is the environmental trigger (which is objective, concrete, and readily discernible) and the emotional response (which is palpable and strongly felt). Transient, nebulous thoughts are usually ignored in the process. (p. 7)

We can add that the same would sometimes hold true for the therapist or counselor. Some practitioners may need to be convinced that a client's beliefs are connected to his or her difficulties, that problems or difficulties are not always attributable to genetics, parenting, the family of origin, childhood experiences, an ill-formed society, or an incompetent government. Instead, before therapists can show clients the impact of beliefs on human emotion and behavior, they must themselves be convinced that to reduce or eliminate negative emotions, clients must first change their beliefs and thinking.

CBT is, as I have noted, the most effective psychotherapeutic intervention for the treatment of generalized anxiety. Its primary focus is on the thinking patterns of the client or, fundamentally, his or her core beliefs. We are therefore in a position to draw the following conclusion: If CBT is the only psychotherapeutic intervention meeting the criteria as an empirically supported treatment for generalized anxiety and if the focus of CBT is on the client's core beliefs, then we may rightly assume that apprehensive expectation and excessive worry are manifestations of one's beliefs about life, the world, self, others, God, and so forth. Said another way, anxiety is directly related to what one believes and does not believe about a given situation. This, of course, has enormous implications for treating the new post–September 11 anxiety, which, when combined with the impact of supermodernity and the inherent difficulty of finding meaning in the overabundance of national and world events, requires from practitioners an intentional focus on the core beliefs of anxious clients. For example, as I illustrate in the following chapter, therapy and counseling, if they are to be effective in treating the new anxiety, must take seriously the core theological beliefs and spiritual values of the client. This is in keeping with the empirical research on CBT and its effectiveness in the treatment of apprehensive expectation about the present and future.

For now, suffice it to say that the essence of cognitive therapy lies in the uncovering and the exploration of the client's core beliefs, or what Aaron Beck has called *protoschemas* (as cited in McMullin, 2000). And as the most effective psychotherapeutic intervention with anxious clients, it means that when treating generalized anxiety or the new anxiety, "cognitive therapy is effective only if the therapist is working on the correct core beliefs." Not that practitioners should feel compelled to uncover and modify core beliefs at the outset of the treatment. This is unwise for several reasons. First, as we know too well, clients are defensive, some massively so, particularly when they are in crisis and feeling anxious and vulnerable. Attempting to uncover the core beliefs of an anxious and vulnerable client at the beginning of the therapy process would be, so to speak, like trying to break into Fort Knox. No doubt the defensiveness on the part of anxious clients has to do with clinging to something, anything that can give a measure of hope and meaning to a crisis situation. But that is not all. Core beliefs are foundational to what the philosopher Edmund Husserl (as cited in Jones, 1980, p. 263) referred to as the *natural standpoint*, the taken-for-granted world of assumptions and presuppositions that we often hold to tenaciously when our lives are threatened or disrupted. The natural standpoint is most often outside the realm of conscious awareness. In Freudian terms, it is making what is unconscious more conscious. In cognitive psychology terms, it is becoming more aware of the automaticity process, the way that we process information and make sense of crisis situations while being on automatic pilot. Whatever framework we decide to apply to the treatment of anxiety—phenomenology, psychoanalysis, cognitive psychology, and so on—it is important to remember that when trying to change beliefs, it is usually best not to work on the core belief first. It is too far away from the client's immediate awareness, and often not acknowledged. It is also more connected to an integrated network of other core beliefs; this makes it far more difficult to extract from the entangled web of beliefs. Cognitive therapists usually work from the surface of the pyramid downward, only tackling core beliefs after the client has shown some skill with the surface thoughts. (McMullin, 2000, pp. 78–80)

The anxious client will not or, more likely, cannot delve immediately into the realm of core beliefs. Practitioners would therefore do well to tickle rather than batter down the particular individual's defenses. McMullin (2000) distinguishes "harder" techniques of countering problematic core beliefs from "softer" techniques. It all depends on what we are treating. For example, more assertive countering techniques that aim "to increase clients' levels of arousal" are the intervention of choice for depressed clients. Assertive countering against a depressive thought or assumption has the potential to help depressed clients

> change not only their thoughts, but also the emotions that accompany them. But there are times when . . . soft emotional techniques, such as calm, relaxed countering, can defuse high emotional arousal and make it easier for clients to more gently change their beliefs.

McMullin has the anxious client in mind when he writes of defusing high emotional arousal. Because harder, more assertive forms of countering core beliefs can accelerate the emotional level of clients, it follows that these intervention techniques can actually cause "anxious clients to become even more fearful. . . . In these cases soft countering is more appropriate." To put this another way,

> for anxiety-producing beliefs, it is often far better to counter in a more relaxed manner. It has been theorized that soft countering reduces the client's state of anxiety, while aggressive countering increases it. In a relaxed state the irrational belief is challenged by both the counter thought and the counter emotion, providing two active treatment elements. (pp. 95, 132)

In working with anxious clients, again, cognitive therapy is the psychotherapeutic treatment of choice with a proven track record. As we have seen, cognitive therapy focuses first and foremost on the client's core belief system and is effective to the extent the therapist is working on the correct core beliefs. However, because of the power of the natural standpoint (the taken-for-granted way of assessing any given situation) combined with the reality of automaticity (the automatic-pilot nature of mental processing), it is best not to work on the core beliefs first but instead work from the surface downward, focusing on the core beliefs after the client has shown enough self-awareness and skill with surface thoughts. This is better facilitated through the application of softer techniques, for example, a calm and relaxed form of countering problematic beliefs and thoughts. A softer form of countering has the capacity to defuse the high emotional arousal of the anxious client and thereby make it easier for him or her to identify, explore, and, if need be, change certain core beliefs that may be doing more harm than good. McMullin (2000) describes the method in a five-step process:

1. Relax your [anxious] clients for five minutes. Give them a transition from their concentration on external events and change their focus to internal events.

2. Turn the client's focus toward the A. Have them imagine as clearly as they can the situation that they are concerned about. Have them use all of their senses (vision, hearing, smell, taste, kinesthetic) to make the A as vivid as they can.

3. While your clients have the A clearly in mind, focus on their C, their emotions. What emotion emerges while imaging A? Ask them not to make up an emotion; let it come in whatever way it comes. Let them feel it.

4. Now ask the clients to focus on their thoughts. Ask them, "What are you telling yourself right now about the A that makes you feel the emotion of C? Let the first thoughts that pop into your mind emerge." If you need to, take a quick break and write the belief [B] down, then return to your clients' mental focusing. (At this point you accept clients' surface beliefs.)

5. Keep their belief clearly in mind and ask clients the questions, "So what if . . . ?" or "Why does it matter that . . . ?" Keep asking the same questions until you find their core answer. It's important to listen to clients' answers and to wait for their imagination to originate a thought. (You may find it useful to write the whole process down in order to help you keep track of your client's answers.) (p. 78)

The Nature of the New Anxiety

Before moving on to chapter 4, I want to sharpen our focus with the new post–September 11 anxiety, specifically from a diagnostic standpoint. To what extent does the new anxiety coincide with the diagnostic criteria for GAD as described in the *DSM–IV–TR*? To what extent does it differ from GAD? Moreover, does the new anxiety require a treatment plan similar to the one I have just outlined? Is cognitive therapy the psychotherapeutic intervention of choice, as it is for generalized anxiety? If so, then the core beliefs of the client become the focus of treatment. As I argue, the new anxiety, a response to an unsettling post–September 11 and supermodern world that we have not yet learned to look at, does stem primarily from what we believe and do not believe about the present and future states of the world. As examined in chapter 2, what is new about post–September 11 living is not that the world has little or no meaning or, when viewed through the lens of postmodernism, has less meaning than it used to. Rather, we now feel an urgent need to invest the world, and not simply our small corner of it, with some sort of explicit meaning. This intense daily need to give meaning to an unrecognized world is, as Augé (1995) suggests, the price we pay for excess, for the overabundance of national and world events so characteristic of supermodern life. The problem is that we are often trying to invest the present world with meaning derived from the past, which is fine but only up to a point. Applying a template of belief and meaning derived from another time and place to a world that we are only beginning to learn how to look at is like trying to insert the proverbial square peg into a round hole. Fear mongerers, in droves, heighten our levels of anxiety by offering us a pessimistic view of the future. Unless we do what they tell us and return to a set of values or a system of belief or meaning largely derived from the past, the future, so they say, does not look very promising. Thus, anxious clients, in this climate of fear, confusion, disorientation, and apprehensive expectation, will need, in the context of therapy and counseling, encouragement and permission to identify, explore, modify, and even change their core sets of beliefs about the present and the future. Practitioners, by focusing on the core beliefs of those in their care, will be in a position to better ascertain whether the belief system of a particular client has the capacity to sustain him or her during this transitional time of momentous change.

Cognitive therapy, with an overt focus on the core beliefs of a client, is uniquely suited to the treatment of post–September 11 anxiety because the new anxiety is a response to the intense daily need to give meaning to the overabundance of pivotal events in our nation and world. But finding meaning in a post–September 11 world characterized by excess or overabundance is easier said than done. Because of the acceleration of time and history and because of the reality of nonplaces superseding place, giving meaning to a world in rapid transition and clarifying one's beliefs about the present and future will prove particularly challenging. With the fleetingness of information about events and issues affecting our world, it may feel as if we are on some sort of treadmill, trying to keep up with what we have heard on the television, what we have seen on the computer, and what we have read in the daily newspaper or weekly news magazine. It is virtually impossible to keep up with the proliferation of information about and analysis of important current events, particularly if it is coming from fear entrepreneurs. By tomorrow, they will have moved on to a completely different set of potential crises and calamities, leaving us to wonder, just as we were beginning to reflect on the meaning of certain events, what became of yesterday's crisis? The fear entrepreneurs, in the interest of effective business, marketing, and politicking, have, by the following day, moved on to other issues, situations, and events but not before they have raised our anxiety level to new heights.

We may, then, rightly conclude that the new anxiety shares certain features and characteristics with GAD. For starters, the new anxiety is characterized by excessive worry about and apprehensive expectation of the events described in chapter 1. The individual finds it difficult, if not impossible, to control or even contain the worry related to, for example, the threat of further terrorism, the sobering implications of global warming, the approaching end of plentiful oil and gasoline without the development of viable alternative energy sources, the rise in immigration and multiculturalism with a simultaneous decline in assimilation, the changing landscape of American employment combined with the outsourcing of jobs overseas, the vanishing middle class, and the potential for America turning into a "house divided." The excessive anxiety is, in and of itself, difficult to control, but the anxiety is then reinforced and exacerbated by the slick maneuvering of political, religious, television, and Internet fear entrepreneurs. Take the media, for example, one of the leading purveyors of analysis and commentary having to do with our post–September 11 world. Exposure to the media, particularly, exposure to those marketing fear under the guise of reporting the news, can and will, over time, have an adverse if not deleterious effect on our overall health and well-being. In the book *In the Wake of 9/11: The Psychology of Terror*, Pyszczynski, Solomon, and Greenberg (2003) write,

> On the one hand, people crave understanding and explanations for the things that have happened to us. They also want to know what might be coming next so they can plan their activities accordingly. Information in times of crisis is essential to the development of understanding.

But the authors continue,

> On the other hand, most people can readily assimilate only so much information. And much of the information presented is redundant and not of much

real use in helping to make sense out of the many facets of the events with which we are struggling. Thus although some level of exposure to the news regarding terrorist attacks and other crises seems essential in facilitating coping, overexposure to the news can actually overwhelm the individual's ability to cope and can lead to exaggerated feelings of fear and hopelessness. (p. 136)

The new anxiety shares with GAD the essential feature of uncontrollable or uncontainable worry and apprehensive expectation. Moreover, the new anxiety, like GAD, is accompanied by additional symptoms, such as restlessness or feeling keyed up or on edge, being easily fatigued, difficulty concentrating or having the mind go blank, irritability, muscle tension, and sleep disturbance (difficulty falling or staying asleep or restless and unsatisfying sleep). There are, however, significant differences between the two diagnoses. GAD, like any other diagnosis listed in the *DSM–IV–TR*, is, as we might expect from a medical model of psychiatry, an individual diagnosis. The *DSM–IV–TR* is, after all, a manual of mental disorders and thus presupposes an autonomous mind at work in an autonomous individual. But the new post–September 11 anxiety is more than simply a mental disorder affecting this individual or that individual. Rather, it is a collective phenomenon affecting a people and a nation, the manifestation of which is in the excessive worry and apprehensive expectation of one who comes to therapy looking for a place to make sense of a world in transition. Practitioners would therefore do well to think outside the box of conventional psychiatric diagnosis, which in no uncertain terms would consider anxiety to be "a manifestation of a behavioral, psychological, or biological dysfunction in the individual" (*DSM–IV*, pp. xxi–xxii). This is, of course, also true of the new anxiety but only up to a point. The new anxiety, simply put, cannot be reduced to a mental problem inside the head of a particular client. In a supermodern post–September 11 world, the new anxiety reflects a collective *disease* with a world that we have not even begun to learn how to look at. To effectively treat the new anxiety, psychotherapists, mental health counselors, and pastoral counselors will need to apply more than a medical and psychiatric diagnosis to the disorder. A comprehensive and systemic approach that situates the new anxiety in a broader national and global framework is just as, or perhaps even more, essential.

There are other differences between the new anxiety and a more generalized form of anxiety. Recall that for generalized anxiety, the worry and apprehensive expectation are not proportionate to the likely occurrence of feared events or, even if the events were to occur, the severity of their impact. Moreover, the worries associated with generalized anxiety may very well arise without any tangible precipitants. The new anxiety, in contrast, arises in response to certain precipitants, even if one has yet to experience their full impact. Should any of these precipitants occur alone or collectively, now or in the future, they will present us with formidable challenges to life as we know it. We can say, on one hand, similar to our assessment of David, that the new anxiety is disproportionate because the precipitants triggering the anxiety have yet to occur or, if they have occurred, have not as of yet affected us with full force. On the other hand, we can say, similar to the way we assessed Jim, that the new anxiety is characterized by more than a little proportionality, for if any or all of the precipants occur, their impact will be greatly and widely felt for generations to come.

Another important difference between generalized anxiety and the new anxiety is that the latter has, as I have been noting, much to do with trying to find meaning in and give meaning to an overabundance of national and world events that, because of the rapid acceleration of time and history, are seemingly here today and gone tomorrow but will more than likely reappear in a day or two or maybe next week or month. This represents a departure from the anxiety described by the existentialists of last century who linked it with the alienation that we are feeling in response to the death of God, that is, the collapse and subsequent loss of meaning. The new post–September 11 anxiety, situated in the context of a supermodern world that we are desperately trying to make sense of, has more to do with trying to give meaning to myriad issues and events that continue to bombard us each and every day. But because supermodern life is characterized by ordeals of solitude and precipitated by the proliferation and the popularity of nonplaces, giving meaning to pivotal current events proves rather difficult. The new anxiety, which each of us experiences to one degree or another, is not the result of the collapse or even the loss of meaning, as postmodernism would suggest. Rather, the new post–September 11 anxiety stems, in large part, from the inability to keep pace with, let alone give meaning to, a world that is leaving us further and further behind. It is here that therapy and counseling become, out of necessity, the place where clients can intentionally step back for a while, away from the madding crowd, and receive the necessary encouragement to go about the business of meaning making (all of which I demonstrate in the following chapter).

Before moving on to chapter 4, where the focus is on working with the anxious client's core beliefs and system of meaning making, I want to systematically outline a working diagnosis for the new anxiety. The diagnostic criteria somewhat overlap the diagnostic features of GAD. There are, however, important differences:

A. Excessive anxiety and worry (apprehensive expectation) about a number of potentially significant issues and events.

B. The client finds it difficult to control or contain the worry.

C. The anxiety and worry are associated with three (or more) of the following symptoms: restlessness or feeling keyed up or on edge, being easily fatigued, difficulty concentrating or having the mind go blank, irritability, muscle tension, and sleep disturbance (difficulty falling or staying asleep or restless and unsatisfying sleep).

D. The anxiety is proportionate to the impact of and subsequent fallout from feared events.

E. The anxiety is triggered not by the collapse or loss of meaning but by the intense daily need to give a rapidly changing world new meaning.

F. The anxiety is exacerbated by the proliferation of nonplaces, which are ultimately illusory.

~

CHAPTER FOUR

The Importance of Assessing Core Theological Beliefs

Therefore do not be anxious about tomorrow, for tomorrow will be anxious for itself. Let the day's own trouble be sufficient for the day.

—Jesus (Matthew 6:34)

If the best available empirically based psychotherapeutic intervention for anxiety is CBT and if the focus of CBT is the belief system of a particular client, then it is important for practitioners to develop a clear understanding of how the individual's beliefs can ameliorate or exacerbate his or her anxiety. A client's beliefs are not, contrary to traditional psychotherapeutic approaches, incidental to the therapeutic process. In fact, in the case of generalized anxiety and, more recently, the new post–September 11 anxiety, what clients believe about themselves, others, God, and life in the present and future will have a direct and fundamental impact on their capacity to cope with an ever-changing world. But again, a client's beliefs, particularly, those that are theological or spiritual, have not always been viewed by practitioners as being essential to the therapeutic treatment. Indeed, from Freud on, beliefs about God, religion, Jesus Christ, and so forth have often been deemed by those working in the fields of psychotherapy and mental health counseling to be, at best, outside the purview of therapy or, at worst, completely irrelevant. With the former group, the client is expected to address his or her theological beliefs in the context of a religious community, preferably with a priest or minister who possesses the requisite theological knowledge and training. The latter group of practitioners, reminiscent of Freud, view the religious faith and theological beliefs of a client as something of an impediment to psychological health and emotional well-being. In either case, the client is expected to check his or her theological beliefs at the door before entering the therapy session. Discussing them with someone else in another setting or not bringing them up at all would seem to be the available options. Depth-oriented psychodynamic approaches tend to keep the focus on the feelings and emotions of a client, on his or her intrapsychic world. A family-systems approach keeps the focus on the client's immediate family, extended family, and family of origin. An object-relations approach keeps the focus on a client's dealings with various objects, that is, the images or mental representations of people in his or her life. Although certain object-relations practitioners (Rizzuto, 1979) have included the topic of God or, specifically, one's god image as a relevant object for discussion in the therapy process, they still seem to be a decided minority.

This is most unfortunate, particularly when it comes to treating the new anxiety. If, as research demonstrates, CBT is the best available empirically based psychotherapeutic intervention for the treatment of anxiety and if CBT focuses on the client's beliefs, then it is incumbent on practitioners to find creative methods for addressing the theological beliefs of their anxious clients. Inviting clients to examine the beliefs that reinforce healthy or unhealthy views and attitudes about self, others, God, and the state of the world is not optional in this new age of anxiety. If the anxious client, for any number of reasons, does not bring up the matter of his or her religious faith, theological beliefs, and spiritual values, if the individual avoids "going there," then the client's therapist or counselor must take the initiative of going there for him or her, of raising the issue for discussion because of its fundamental importance in the treatment of anxiety. In this new age of anxiety, when the traditional places of meaning making have been supplanted by the proliferation of nonplaces, therapy and counseling have the potential of offering to clients a unique place for disclosing, addressing, revising, or changing one's beliefs about life and the world. Recall that more and more Americans prefer to describe themselves as being spiritual rather than religious, which is all well and good until we pause to reflect on the double-edgedness of this trend. On one hand, the need to be "spiritual" highlights the quest of many Americans to find a life-giving faith that is not bogged down by myriad layers of tradition, doctrine, and dogma. On the other hand, it also highlights, as Augé (1995) would surely point out, yet another solitary endeavor, which suggests that spirituality divorced from place has the potential of morphing into another nonplace. For psychotherapists, mental health practitioners, and pastoral counselors to effectively treat the new anxiety, they will need to be intentional about creating the space or, to use Augé's word, the *place* where anxious clients are encouraged to delve fully and meaningfully into their theological beliefs and spiritual values.

This chapter addresses the importance of beliefs, particularly, theological beliefs, in the treatment of the new anxiety. But, again, bringing the client's theology and religious faith into the treatment process has been, for quite some time, a point of contention within the psychotherapeutic community. Fortunately, this has begun to change as more practitioners see the need to treat the whole person rather than certain aspects of the person—for example, feelings, grief, thoughts, relationships, and so on. This trajectory of greater openness toward the theological beliefs and spiritual values of clients parallels the shift that we have seen in the medical community, as more physicians are not only improving their listening skills and so-called bedside manner but also taking seriously the religious and spiritual lives of their patients. Still, the number of psychotherapeutic and mental health practitioners who see the importance of addressing and exploring the theology of anxious clients remains an unambiguous minority. One reason has to do with the therapist's or counselor's level of comfort with religious faith and spiritual practice in general and with the degree of clarity about his or her own belief system in particular. It is more than a little naïve to think, even in the case of the secular therapist who seemingly does not subscribe to any organized system of belief, that a theological framework for viewing the world is reserved for those less enlightened or for those chronic worriers who need a "crutch," or a coping device, lest their anxiety get the better of them. Everyone, even the educated and enlightened practitioner, believes in something. Thus, preparatory to helping anxious clients identify and explore their beliefs about God, life, and the present and future states of the world, the therapist or counselor needs to reflect intentionally on his or her own beliefs about the same phenomena: God, life, and whether they view the present and the future with a sense of hopefulness or pessimism.

The theology of the practitioner—whether conventional or unconventional, organized or eclectic, informed by a traditional religious faith community or not—is not insignificant when it comes to treating the new anxiety. In fact, as I argue in this chapter, practitioners, in addition to becoming clear about their personal belief systems, can at times introduce into the therapy process their own core beliefs, if done carefully and appropriately. This, I am well aware, is a departure from traditional psychotherapeutic theory and practice and may make certain practitioners rather nervous. If truth be told, it makes me a little nervous to consider the pros and cons of practitioners' introducing their theology into the counseling session. In fact, I devote part of the next chapter to the dangers of imposing one's belief system onto unsus-pecting clients, given the power differential between therapist and client. For now, though, in the remaining pages of this particular chapter, I wish to dis-cuss the pros of (a) encouraging anxious clients to reflect on and examine core beliefs that have the potential to calm or trigger their anxiety and worry and (b) modeling for clients how to go about reflecting, theologically, on the myriad pressing issues of the day. For those practitioners who find themselves skeptical of my methodology, who are considering putting down the book and reading no further, I urge them to reconsider the centrality of core the-ological beliefs in light of the treatment of the new anxiety. With the find-ings that CBT is the best available empirically based psychotherapeutic in-tervention for generalized anxiety and, by extension, the new post–September 11 anxiety, that CBT is the only psychotherapeutic ap-proach meeting criteria as an empirically supported treatment for anxiety, therapy or counseling that overlooks, ignores, or glosses over the core theo-logical beliefs of an anxious client will certainly be suspect in terms of its ef-fectiveness. Moreover, in this era of supermodernity, it begs the question, where does the client go to make sense of a rapidly changing world if he or she is prohibited, directly or indirectly, from doing so in the therapy session? With whom, if not the therapist, can the anxious client disclose, explore, re-vise, and even change certain core theological beliefs that have the poten-tial for providing him or her with a measure of authentic hope about the pres-ent and the future or reinforcing a fear-based outlook on life? With the decline in religious practice being illustrative of not the collapse of meaning but rather the reality of established places of meaning making giving way to the proliferation of solitary nonplaces, it falls to the psychotherapist and counselor to serve as a priest, minister, or shaman of sorts when it comes to exploring questions about God, theology, and the meaning and purpose of life.

A Therapeutic Misstep

A number of years ago, during my clinical training, I and other members of my training group viewed a videotape of a counseling session with an anx-ious and depressed client. A middle-aged woman, the client was still, several years later, trying to come to terms with the tragic death of her young son. While the mother was not looking, the boy had dashed out into the street and was struck and killed by a car. She could not forgive herself for having looked away at the precise moment that her son ran out into the street. If only, she lamented, she had been a better mother, if only she had been more on top of things, if only she had paid more attention to her son, he would still be alive today. It was heartbreaking to listen to her story, for she was, after all, locked in a vicious cycle of perpetual grief, anxiety, and depression. The practitioner in the tape empathically met the client where she was, in the depths of her pain and grief. Moreover, the therapist skillfully helped the client to pinpoint the secondary gain of her depression, which had become a form of "perpetual penance" for the "sin" of having failed her son. By remaining stuck in her grief and depression, the women, albeit negatively, was maintaining an emotional attachment to the deceased boy. But then came a pivotal moment in the counseling session, which the therapist either missed or ignored. The grieving mother gave her caregiver a glimpse into her anxiety as she intimated that she was greatly concerned about her son's present whereabouts, whether the boy was safely in the hands of God and whether God could be trusted to care for him. The therapist acknowledged the client's concern about God, albeit briefly and superficially, and then went on to tell her that he was more interested in hearing her talk about herself than about God and the afterlife. Not that he discounted her belief in God or ridiculed her theology of heaven and eternal life. Not at all. His therapeutic misstep was more subtle than that and more than likely went unnoticed by the majority of students and training supervisors. In the treatment of anxiety (not to mention depression), CBT, with its proven track record, challenges us to give more weight to the core beliefs of a client, including those that are theological. If we are practicing a client-centered cognitive–behavioral approach to the treatment of anxiety, then the matter of core beliefs, including those having to do with God and the afterlife, must be explored in depth rather than glossed over. For this particular client, it amounted to ignoring the very ground of her being.

In this videotape session, the client was able to identify several important issues linked to the perpetuation of her grief and depression. For example, she was able to acknowledge that remaining stuck in the pain was a form of penance, although she conceded to the therapist that her doing penance would have no end, because this would mean that she would have to forgive herself—and she was not about to forgive herself for having looked away at the precise moment that her son ran out into the street. The client, with the skillful help of the therapist, was also able to see that staying stuck in her pain, grief, and depression was a way for her to remain connected to her deceased son, a way for her to keep from having to say goodbye to him and acknowledge that she needed to let him go and thus move on with her life. In certain ways, the question Jesus asked of the lame man at the pool of Bethesda (John 5:6) would be apropos to the situation of this client: Do you want to get well? As she admitted to the therapist, a part of her did not want to get well, because in getting well, she would lose the emotional connection with her son. All well and good. But the treatment, at least the therapy that we saw in the videotape session, did not take seriously enough the woman's beliefs and theology about God and the afterlife. The therapist was either not prepared to deal with the client's theology or, worse, not all that interested. In either case, the anxiety that this individual was experiencing went untreated because it stemmed from her core beliefs about the nature of God, life after death, and whether God can be trusted to care for her son in the next world.

The client in this vignette would have left the counseling session with greater insight and understanding about herself and her relationship with her deceased son. Her relationship with God, however, went unexamined, which is most unfortunate because what she believes about the nature of God and the nature of the afterlife will be a source of hope and healing or a source of greater anxiety. The therapist did not encourage the woman to address, let alone explore, her beliefs about God and whether God has the capacity to care for her son. In fact, the therapist was rather dismissive of her theology, albeit subtly, which prompted the client, out of deference to the counselor, to return to issues that she felt were more important to him. What she believes about God, however, is fundamentally related to her present level of anxiety and whether she feels her anxiety as being manageable or not. One does not have to be a trained psychotherapist or theologian to intuit that this mother struggles to find authentic hope and meaning in the face of the tragic loss of her son. Questions that she must be pondering include the following: What kind of God would cause or, at the very least, allow a precious little boy to run out into the street and be struck and killed by a car? What kind of God would let a mother look away, just for an instant, at precisely the moment that her young son darts out into the street? What kind of God allows young and tender lives to be snuffed out even before they have had a chance to experience the richness and depth of life? Does God even care? If God let her down when she and her son needed God the most, then how can she trust God to care for her son in the afterlife? Who is to say the boy is being loved and cared for, or is he once again being subjected to the winds of fate, chance, and circumstance? What this demonstrates, of course, is that there is another layer of experience waiting to be explored, a layer of belief and theology that relates to the client's present level of anxiety. By not inviting the client to "go there," by not addressing more earnestly her beliefs about the nature of God, the existence of an afterlife, and life after death, the therapist was, in a sense, communicating to this client that it would be better for her to leave her theology outside of the counseling room.

In the remaining pages of this chapter, I develop a framework for treating the new anxiety that is based on the empirical finding that a cognitive–behavioral approach to anxiety is the treatment of choice and that, because CBT focuses on core beliefs, the core theological beliefs of a client must be taken seriously. This presupposes, in the interest of treating anxiety as effectively as possible, openness on the part of practitioners to the religious or spiritual life of the client, what we might describe as a holy or even sacred curiosity. To be sure, treating the new anxiety requires more than the traditional stance of therapeutic neutrality. It even requires more than the stance of "being with" the client, as articulated by self-psychology. Being with those in our care, from the perspective of self-psychology, has meant being fully present with the client, a welcome departure from a traditional psychoanalytic approach, which urges practitioners to always keep their emotional distance, lest clients become passive, dependent, and deferential. There is certainly the danger that in empathically immersing ourselves into the life of a client that the individual may become too dependent on our knowledge, expertise, and emotional strength. The far greater danger, however, is that in keeping our emotional distance from those in our care, in modeling ourselves after the emotionless surgeon, as Freud suggested, such therapy may have the effect of leaving clients feeling emotionally abandoned and wondering if their caregivers really do care. Kohut (as cited in Cooper-White, 2004), in quoting Freud, argued that "certain analysts . . . did indeed oppose the attitude of 'the surgeon, who puts aside all his feelings, even his human sympathy,' as he proceeds to drain the pathogenic abscess in the unconscious." Kohut goes on to say that "through self psychology, the analyst acquires the ability to be empathic with the patient's inner experience of himself as part of the analyst or of the analyst as part of himself." Therapy and counseling become, as it were, a deeply empathic form of reparenting:

> We must never confuse the deep human response called forth in us vis-à-vis another human being's thoughts and emotions with sentimentality and companionship. Parents and analysts, respectively, will insist on the child's and the analysand's confronting unpleasant realities, including the limits that all of us have to recognize, but they will do so while simultaneously acknowledging the facts that all of us rightfully feel special and unique and that we cannot exist unless we feel that we are affirmed by others, including, and especially by our parents and those who later come to have a parental selfobject significance for us. (pp. 113, 173, 190)

"Being with" the client, as put forward by self-psychology, means total empathic immersion into the emotional world of the person in our care. For the client to grow, change, and experience healing in the treatment process, he or she must feel unconditionally accepted and understood by the caregiver. Acceptance, empathy, and understanding can be conveyed by way of appropriate self-disclosure on the part of the caregiver, again, representing a healthy departure from more traditional or classical forms of psychoanalysis. For example, the therapist or counselor, in being fully present with the client and emphatically immersed in the person's pain, suffering, and confusion, can, in the interest of therapeutic effectiveness and rapport, share what the experience of listening to the client's story is evoking. The therapist may give empathic feedback by saying something to the effect of "I feel sad when I hear you describe that situation," "It angers me to hear how they treated you," or, as in the case of Jim, "I feel anxious when I hear you describe your financial situation." The therapist can even go further with the self-disclosure by sharing, appropriately, briefly, and succinctly, something from personal experience that might have the potential of resonating with the client. The practitioner must guard against disclosing too much personal information, which could lead to role reversal in the sense that the client becomes caregiver to the therapist. The dangers of overdependence, passivity, and role reversal notwithstanding, the greater danger lies in not being fully present with the totality of the client's experience, as well as in not sharing anything of one's self, even when called for by the therapy situation. For the practitioner to encourage a client to bring the totality of self into therapy while keeping one's own self outside the counseling room communicates something of a mixed message. I am not at all advocating that therapy become some sort of informal coffee talk between friends. Rather, through the appropriate sharing of self in the counseling process, the therapist helps the client to feel accepted and understood not just intellectually but, more important, empathically and emotionally, even spiritually. Put another way, the client feels as if the therapist "gets" him or her, as if the caregiver fully understands the client's emotional and spiritual truth.

What are the implications for the treatment of the new anxiety? For starters, one cannot effectively treat the new anxiety without the use of self in the counseling process, without extending to the client genuine empathy, emotional availability, and appropriate self-disclosure. Self-psychology has served as a corrective to traditional forms of psychoanalysis, reminding us, apropos to the treatment of anxiety, that adopting the attitude of a surgeon, who puts aside feelings, emotions, and human sympathy and empathy, will make the anxious client feel even more anxious and uncertain. But that is not all. When it comes to treating the new anxiety, the use of self on the part of the therapist must, at times, include a willingness to disclose what one believes about God, a world in transition, the pressing issues of the day, and so on. The new anxiety reflects the urgent and intense daily need to give new meaning, any meaning, to a world that is rapidly changing right before our eyes. As we saw with the therapist in the training videotape, if certain beliefs of a client, particularly, those of a theological nature, are ignored, minimized, or not taken all that seriously, then the client has little opportunity to explore the foundations of his or her meaning making, a prerequisite to the effective treatment of both generalized anxiety and the new anxiety. Nor will the therapist be able to disclose what he or she believes about the issues being discussed, which means, unfortunately, that the client is left hanging and is now on his or her own when it comes to sorting through a potentially convoluted belief system. Although we must remember that CBT, rather than self-psychology, is the treatment of choice for anxiety, we can nevertheless see an important connection between the two modalities: The use of self, mandated by self-psychology, is now extended to the belief systems of practitioners who, when working with the new post–September 11 anxiety, must, in keeping with CBT, fully immerse themselves in the core beliefs of their clients.

What is being conveyed is that in treating the new anxiety, the use of self becomes, out of necessity, extended to the theology and belief system of the therapist or counselor. The task of the practitioner is twofold: first, encourage anxious clients to bring the totality of themselves, including their core theological beliefs, into the counseling session and, second, be prepared to disclose, appropriately and succinctly, one's own beliefs relevant to the issues at hand. This, as I have stated, requires great care and skill, for there is always the risk of imposing our beliefs and theology on an anxious client. Again, I address this potential danger in the next chapter. For now, it is important for practitioners to see that when caring for the anxious, it is necessary to include in the cognitive–behavioral category of core beliefs the religious and theological views of the client. Although this certainly applies to the treatment of anxiety in general, I argue that it applies even more so to the treatment of the new anxiety. Recall that the new anxiety is situated in a supermodern and post–September 11 world, where there is no shortage of apprehensive expectation about the present and the future. Life in this supermodern context moves at such an accelerated pace that it leaves us breathless, unable to stay abreast of all the momentous current events, let alone give them any kind of significant and lasting meaning. The therapy session, interestingly enough, becomes the relational place where anxious men and women can go to make sense of an ever-changing world. In this age of anxiety, when many of us are struggling to find some measure of meaning in the world around us, psychotherapy, with the decline of formal religious practice, must be willing to fill the void. We might even say—and I am not being hyperbolic—that therapy and counseling, when treating the new anxiety, can be a form of sacred space for the practitioner so inclined. The therapist in the training videotape had this opportunity, but because of a disinclination toward theological language and beliefs, he steered the client away from what was more than likely her core belief and, from an ontological standpoint, quite possibly her very ground of being.

What, we might ask, would have made this practitioner respond differently to his client? What would have motivated him to be more respectful of the client's core belief in God and her intense and urgent need to sort out whether God does in fact love us and care for us and whether God is caring for her son in the afterlife? True, the session may have gone in a completely different direction from what we saw on the videotape, but this would not necessarily have been a bad thing. The mother wanted, actually needed, to address the issue of her son's being eternally in the hands and care of God, but the practitioner steered her away from a potentially meaningful and pivotal discussion. If the therapist had been treating the new anxiety, then the intervention to steer this client away from theology and her core beliefs about God and the afterlife would have been even more unfortunate. Maybe the therapist was uncomfortable in the area of "God talk," or maybe he was, so to speak, out of his element, never having received adequate or even possibly any theological preparation during his clinical training. As William Miller (1999) points out in *Integrating Spirituality Into Treatment*, "clinical training programs typically do little to prepare their students for professional roles with people who vary widely in their spiritual and religious backgrounds, an oversight that has been pointed out for decades." The oversight is even more glaring in the new age of anxiety, where more and more clients are seeking a place to find renewed meaning and authentic hope for the present and the future. Miller goes on to say that

> the problem has been, in part, a shortage within training programs of role models for such integration. As a group, mental health professionals in general and psychologists in particular tend to report low levels of religious belief and involvement relative to the U.S. population. The historical reasons for this are unclear, but this underrepresentation serves to pass on a deficit in sensitivity from generation to generation of psychotherapists. This is one reason why religious laity and professionals have sometimes been wary of referring to mental health professionals. (p. 254)

For religious professionals and clergy who would view this videotape, the concern would surely arise about the capacity of this practitioner and, by extension, others working in the field of psychotherapy to demonstrate sensitivity toward and respect for the religious values and theological beliefs of parishioners.

Treating the new anxiety, which results from living within the convergence of supermodernity and a post–September 11 world, requires from practitioners a reorientation toward the core beliefs of those in their care. Specifically, it requires an openness toward and even a holy curiosity about the religious views and theological beliefs of a client that fill the individual with a sense of hope and peace or a deep sense of apprehension and foreboding about the present and the future. Not that the therapist or counselor needs to be a trained theologian or clergyperson to engage the client about his or her core theological beliefs and system of meaning making. Nor does the practitioner have to share the client's theological perspective and religious views or even be a religious believer for that matter. What treating the new anxiety does require, however, is a profound respect for religious belief and diversity. The anxious client's beliefs about, for example, God, Jesus Christ, and God's involvement in the world and in the person's life matter greatly in the formation of meaning and how it becomes applied in daily living. In fact, the how is just as or maybe more important than the what. Put another way, how the client applies his or her personal theology to difficult and challenging situations will give the therapist important clues about the capacity of the person's belief system to sustain him or her during anxious times. The therapist in the training videotape caught a glimpse of what the client believed about God and the afterlife yet, for reasons known only to him, neglected to ask her to expand on these core beliefs. By avoiding the specifics of her beliefs, the what of her theological views, the practitioner missed a valuable opportunity to explore how the belief system of the client reduces or increases her level of anxiety. Again, one does not have to be a trained theologian, an ordained clergyperson, or technically even a believer to help anxious clients explore their core theological beliefs. "Just as one does not need to be a recovering alcoholic or drug addict to treat substance use disorders effectively . . . one needs not be a believer to help clients discuss spiritual features of their condition and care." This should put the caregiver at ease, particularly, the practitioner who wonders, "What if I do not share the client's spiritual perspective or religious belief system?" The fact is that

> psychologists, physicians, and scientists are not representatives of the populations they serve when it comes to spiritual beliefs and religious involvement. . . .

A specialist's approach would be to call in qualified clergy to deal with spiritual aspects of a client's care, and there are distinct advantages to interprofessional collaboration. Yet, as already noted, clients generally do not want to be understood just in parts but as a whole person, and we believe . . . that all health care providers should know something of their clients' spirituality to develop a comprehensive understanding of their problems and design an appropriate treatment plan. (Miller, 1999, p. 12)

Taking the Core Beliefs of Clients Seriously

The training videotape serves as an important reference point vis-à-vis the treatment of anxiety and the fundamental significance of the anxious client's core beliefs. True, the therapist was dealing with several presenting issues, most notably, depression caused by unresolved grief. Regrettably, what was not addressed was the client's anxiety about her son's whereabouts in the afterlife and whether God could be trusted to care for the boy in her absence. The case vignette serves as an example of how and how not to go about treating the new post–September 11 anxiety, which I address in the remaining pages of this chapter. It is important to understand the rationale for intentionally bringing into the treatment process the core religious and theological beliefs of any client, especially, the client who is anxious. In contrast to the vignette from the training videotape, I offer a vignette from Agneta Schreurs's *Psychotherapy and Spirituality* (2002). The client in this case study has also suffered the most devastating of all losses, the loss of a child. But in contrast to the previous case, we see Schreurs making all kinds of important connections between the psychological and spiritual issues of the case. The contrasting case studies serve as an important foundation for the development of a systematic approach to the core theological beliefs of the anxious client. I quote at length her commentary on the brief vignette:

One of my patients, a woman of about 40 years old, has lost a child in a car accident. She is a member of a small Protestant church. She is convinced that the death of her child is a punishment of God, because she has been unfaithful to her husband. How am I to approach this?

The interconnection of psychological and spiritual aspects is very clear here. Like so many parents mourning a child's death, this woman probably suffers from irrational guilt feelings. Her theology allows her to rationalize these feelings falsely by connecting the accident with her real guilt of adultery. It is quite clear, first, that this theology is a serious obstacle for any psychological healing. It is also quite clear that it is a serious obstacle for any spiritual healing. Who could ever love and trust a God who is prepared to kill a child to punish the parent? It is bad theology too. In the Bible, there are indeed texts about the wrath of God and punishment. But these texts are abundantly nuanced and counter-balanced by a great variety of texts emphasizing his compassion and forgiveness for whomever sincerely repents. Why didn't this woman apply these to herself? And she is no exception as a "religious person" in not doing so.

If she were to communicate her feelings to the [therapy] group, then this might be an opportunity to separate the pernicious bond between her and her guilt. But how are therapists to use this opportunity? Aren't we supposed to re-spect the individual or group religions? Who are we (as therapists) to pass judg-ment on any theology whatsoever?

As a therapist, you are not in a position to judge religious truths. Nor would you be likely to have them discussed in your groups, as this would too easily di-vert the group's attention from their real work. However, whenever religious or spiritual issues emerge in therapy you have to deal with *significant individual-and group-generated versions*, and you will feel the need to assess *their* therapeu-tic significance. With this in mind I think it is useful to distinguish in your own mind (albeit somewhat artificially) between the person's relationship with God on the one hand and cognitive structuring on the other. The latter is where cultural root metaphors enter the picture. Religious cognitive systems may or may not be based on inflexible and absolute root metaphors. But if they are, this may be a serious obstacle both for therapeutic and spiritual growth. But do not lose sight of the fact that an individual's or group's authentic search for a harmonious relationship with God may still be present, which in turn is favor-able for therapeutic and spiritual growth.

Looking at such cases from the viewpoint of cultural root metaphors may well provide a handle on how to deal with such religious obstacles to therapy. It enables us to see for example that this woman in [the vignette] has been making the mechanistic root metaphor absolute and thereby into an ideology, that is, a closed cognitive system. With that closed system, there can be no other role for God than the leading role in linking causes to their appropriate linear effects. Unfortunately, in most cases such insights cannot be used di-rectly in a therapeutic intervention. Too many people would be prone to think that you are attacking their faith. But there is another way. You could try to ex-plore, first, whether the patient is indeed organizing the rest of her life in the same linear way, and second, whether perhaps the whole group is or is not or-ganizing itself by this mechanistic metaphor which they too have made ab-solute. Are the group members always looking backwards for external, earlier causes of their trouble, or always trying to find a scapegoat whenever their in-teraction gets out of hand? Could it be the group matrix that triggered and is reinforcing this woman's interpretation of her loss? In the event that your ob-servation would confirm one or other or both of these hypotheses, you can un-doubtedly find a way to work at changing or making more flexible this under-lying organizing principle, at the individual and/or at the collective level. To do so would bring about a second-order change, which in its turn would probably trigger off a gradual change in both theological thinking and feeling. (pp. 94–95)

The contrast between the two cases could not be more striking. In the training videotape, the therapist gives lip service to the client's need to address the "God issue" as it relates to her son's existence in the afterlife. In fact, he throws something of a roadblock up, telling her in no uncertain terms that he is far more interested in what she thinks and feels about her son's tragic death than in what she believes God thinks about all of this. Had the therapist taken more seriously the theology of the client, he might have discovered, as in the second vignette, not only an obstacle to but also a resource for the client's psychological and spiritual healing and renewal. Quite possibly, his client, like the women in the second case study, was locked into a religious cognitive system based on inflexible and absolute root metaphors. Perhaps, she, too, or at least part of her believes that the death of her son was a form of punishment from God, for something that she had done or not done, for "sin" as it were. Maybe if the therapist had invited her to expand on her core theological beliefs about God, she, like the client in the second vignette, would have had the opportunity to "get something off her chest." Because of the second practitioner's intentional approach to reflecting theologically on her client's core beliefs about God, the door was opened to probe even further about other important beliefs, such as sin, punishment, and cause and effect, beliefs that were preventing her from experiencing psychological and spiritual growth and healing. The second brief vignette illustrates that therapy, particularly with anxious clients, becomes a quasi confessional in the presence of the practitioner. In the second vignette, we see that the client must "confess" her sin of infidelity before she can ever hope to begin healing psychologically and spiritually and before she can begin the process of reconstructing a flexible and healthier theological belief system. Whether the client in the first vignette needed to confess anything of a religious nature, whether her theological belief system had the capacity for healing and integration or a capacity to judge and condemn, we will unfortunately never know.

The two case vignettes contrastingly illustrate the need to be clear about what we are dealing with when it comes to the core theological beliefs of a client. This is true for psychotherapeutic work in general but even more so when we are caring for the anxious. Recall the empirical findings that CBT is the best available psychotherapeutic intervention for anxiety and that the major focus of CBT is the core beliefs of a client. The core beliefs include beliefs about self, others, relationships, difficult situations, tragic sets of circumstances, success, failure, gain, loss, and so on. Added to and moved to-ward or near the top of this list, apropos to the new post–September 11 anx-iety, are the core theological beliefs of anxious clients. The new anxiety is a response to the fears and apprehension of living in a post–September 11 world, as well as a response to the excesses of supermodernity: the accelera-tion of time, the overabundance of national and world events, the prolifer-ation of nonplaces, and the difficulty attaching meaning to a world that seems more complicated and confusing with each passing day. Clients are wondering, individually and collectively, where is God in all of this, in a post–September 11 world characterized by a pervasive anxiety about the present and the future, fueled by excessive fearmongering in newspapers, on nighttime cable television, and over the Internet? Does God care about a nation and world in transition and crisis, particularly, this nation, which prides itself in being a leader in world affairs and, for some, a moral and re-ligious beacon? Is there tangible and credible hope for the present and fu-ture? What kind of world will our children and grandchildren inherit from us? A world that is better or worse off than the one we know? All of these questions deal with theology in one form or another. To avoid "going there," ostensibly because the client's religious faith and theological beliefs are con-sidered to be, in traditional psychotherapeutic terms, not relevant to the treatment, does a great disservice to anxious clients and demonstrates a lack of understanding about the new anxiety.

The problem is that for some psychotherapists and mental health coun-selors, there is incredulity about the necessity of including theological beliefs in the treatment process, even for anxiety, whereas for others it is more of a lack of training in how to go about engaging clients in the task of theologi-cal reflection. Again, practitioners and mental health professionals do not need a degree in religion or theology or an ordination credential to help clients sort through their core beliefs. Rather, what is required is simply a genuine respect for the theological views and religious beliefs of those in our care. For the former group of practitioners, those who view theology and re-ligious beliefs as being pathogenic or irrelevant or both, there is need to think outside the box of traditional psychotherapeutic learning and training. At one time, maybe, it was fashionable to keep theology out of the counsel-ing room, but now, in an age of pervasive anxiety, that therapeutic stance has the potential to do more harm than good. The critique of the Enlighten-ment, with its emphasis on the scientific method and on rationality and rea-son, combined with the pejorative assessment of religious faith that comes to us by way of classical Freudian and psychoanalytic theory, has had an enormous impact on the field of psychology and on the disciplines of psychotherapy, mental health counseling, and, surprisingly enough, pastoral counseling. Frame (2003), citing several studies from the early 1990s, writes,

That a large number of counselors have negative feelings about religion may contribute to their difficulty in dealing with religious clients. In a national study of mental health providers, only 29% believed that clients' religious and spiritual issues were appropriate areas to be addressed in therapy. . . . In addition, researchers found that in a national sample of clinical psychologists' religious and spiritual orientations, 25% expressed negative feelings about past religious involvement. . . . Thus, it is likely that counselors might have a disapproving or cynical reaction to religious clients. . . . There are a number of reasons that, until recently, psychotherapy and religion have been bifurcated. (p. 16)

The second group of practitioners, those who demonstrate sensitivity toward the core theological beliefs and spiritual values of clients but at the same time lack the necessary training in how to integrate theological reflection into the counseling process, will need remedial help in how to go about engaging clients in the area of core spiritual and theological beliefs. It is important to remember that because great care and skill are needed when working with the core beliefs of a client, not just anyone can help an individual identify, explore, revise, and, if need be, change beliefs that are foundational to his or her system of meaning making. In some ways, it is reminiscent of the art of listening. Anyone, it is true, can listen to what another person is saying, but not everyone can hear what is being communicated on multiple levels. The therapist in the training videotape was particularly skillful at helping the client work through her unresolved grief and to see how in many ways it reinforced her depression. But while listening to her theological views about God and the afterlife, he did not hear how these core theological beliefs could be fundamentally related to the anxiety that she was experiencing as she pondered the nature of God, God's capacity to care for her son in the next life, whether there is an actual afterlife, and if she will ever see her son again. Giving the therapist the benefit of the doubt, we can say that he was not at all opposed to bringing the core theological beliefs of his client into the treatment process. Rather, he simply lacked a framework for doing so. Thus, whether we neglect the core theological beliefs of a client intentionally or unintentionally because we are opposed to their inclusion in the treatment process or because we do not feel confident enough "going there," the result is the same:

The spiritual is then in danger of being split off. . . . For [the client] it is quite often simultaneously a vital lifeline to the Transcendent, and/or to the community into which he is socialized. In such a circumstance it is more urgent than ever that religion and spirituality do not split off as separate realms.

Schreurs (2002) goes on to ask, "But what can be done to prevent a split-off from arising when the therapist for a good reason has decided deliberately to move away from approaching a theology issue directly?" She offers the discerning therapist and counselor a practical strategy:

> Maybe moments of silent reflection could be made a standard procedure in each session? After analyzing and working through whatever has occurred at the psychological or interpersonal level, the therapist might then insert an integrative phase. In that part of the session, each individual group member could be invited to consider silently whether what has just happened in the group sheds light on how he personally relates to others outside the group, God included. In that way integrating new insights into the spiritual realm will not be something special, but a natural part of the process. (pp. 226–227)

Schreurs is situating the discussion into the context of group therapy, but her insights about avoiding a "split-off" in the treatment process could just as effectively be applied to the treatment of anxiety in general and to the new post–September 11 anxiety in particular. How so? Recall that the new anxiety is a response to a rapidly changing world and the difficulty in making sense of or giving meaning to an overabundance of national and global events. As Augé (1995) points out, the difficulty is not so much with, as postmodernists see it, the collapse or loss of meaning but rather with the overinvestment of meaning, the price that we pay for the essential features of supermodernity: excess, change, and the proliferation of nonplaces. When supermodernity collides with the reality of a post–September 11 world, then what we can expect as practitioners is an increase in the incidence and levels of anxiety combined with a deep hunger for meaning and understanding. We see the manifestation of this in the dramatic increase in spirituality in America. People, those in our care, are looking for answers, something to believe in and ground their lives in at a time when the forces all around them threaten to thwart the very processes of meaning making. It is important that anxious clients not be thwarted in their quest to believe and find meaning by practitioners who intentionally or unintentionally steer them away from religious and theological issues. If CBT is the treatment of choice for the new anxiety, then this particular therapeutic modality, which focuses on the core beliefs of a client, should remind us that we are fundamentally obligated to "go there" with our clients into the depths of their theology and spirituality.

Becoming more comfortable with the core theological beliefs of anxious clients will prevent what Schreurs calls a "split-off" from occurring. It must be remembered that at any point of human history, but even more so in an age of apprehensive expectation about the present and the future, one's core theological beliefs become a vital lifeline to the Transcendent, something that the therapist or counselor must take seriously. For some practitioners, this is not a problem. For others, it will take some getting used to, especially if they have bought into certain presuppositions coming from Freud, Marx, and anyone else who views religious faith exclusively through a pathogenic lens. Whether the presupposition is that religion is a illusion (that which retards the intellectual and emotional development of the human species) or the opiate of the people (that which numbs the pain of our suffering), what results is a rather dogmatic and one-sided interpretation of religion that can cloud our judgment about its efficaciousness in the life of the anxious client. A cognitive–behavioral therapeutic approach to the treatment of the new anxiety has the capacity to meaningfully engage the client in the area of core theological beliefs, helping one distinguish those beliefs that are beneficial in terms of coping with daily living from those that are not. What this approach manages to do is to keep practitioners from developing their own form of splitting, seeing religious beliefs and theological views as either an all-good object or, more likely, an all-bad object. To adopt a view of religious faith as something that is all bad and exclusively pathogenic says, in a Rorschacian sort of way, a great deal more about the mind-set of the mental health professional than it does about a client or the nature of religion and spirituality. Schreurs rightly points out that it has become a necessity to think in terms of an integrative phase of therapy that, after taking into consideration the psychological and interpersonal issues of a case, invites the anxious client to explore the core theological beliefs that underlie his or her system of meaning making. In so doing, the therapist and client will together be able to see more clearly "the ways in which beliefs about the transcendent are involved in the coping process, specifically how these beliefs affect the search for control." For example, with God viewed "as a partner in the coping process," we see how "the person works with God to find meaning in difficult situations, to generate and implement solutions to problems, and to sustain the self emotionally" (Miller, 1999, pp. 181–182).

A more nuanced and sophisticated approach to core theological beliefs is necessary to treat the new anxiety effectively. If there is any therapeutic neutrality on the part of the therapist or counselor, it has to do with keeping an open mind about what specific theological views "could be used as resources in treatment and which ones could be contributing to the problem" (Frame,

2003, p. 98). What this means, in practical terms, is that practitioners must guard against any tendency to pathologize or relativize religious faith. For those who have difficulty seeing any inherent value in religion or spiritual-ity, it would do them well to stop and remember that

> a large body of correlational research documents a generally positive relation-ship between religious involvement and health outcomes, including mental health. Other studies have shown that with religiously committed clients, the effectiveness of psychotherapy can be increased when their beliefs are not only respected but also actively incorporated in treatment regardless of the thera-pist's own belief. (Miller, 1999, p. 255)

However, for those practitioners who tend to view religion and spirituality more relativistically—that is, one form of religious or spiritual expression is as good as another—it would do them well to recall that a relativistic therapeu-tic stance with an anxious client will exacerbate the individual's feeling of ap-prehensive expectation about the present and the future. The new anxiety, to be sure, is a response to the precariousness of post–September 11 living as well as to the challenges of supermodernity, most notably, the difficulty attaching any sort of lasting meaning to a world characterized by excessive change and transition. Thus, to convey directly or indirectly to anxious clients that one set of theological beliefs is as good as the other is to leave them

> pondering whether that on which they have based their whole sense of mean-ing and value is, in William James's words, a "mere mask, a tissue spun in happy hours." How secure, then, can we be? Well, without our martinis, marijuana, cocaine, Prozac, Zoloft, Paxil, and so on, it appears not very. (Pyszczynski et al., 2003, p. 197)

In a supermodern post–September 11 world, therapy and counseling must become integrative of core theological beliefs and the task of meaning mak-ing, particularly when caring for the anxious. This is no longer optional, as if people have an assortment of other venues for addressing their spiritual con-cerns and theological views about the nature of God, the extent of God's in-volvement in the world, what kind of world our children and their children will inherit, and the capacity of human resourcefulness to make the future world a better place. Where else, in a supermodern world characterized by the proliferation of nonplaces, can people seek guidance in sorting through these important questions? The church or synagogue? Recall that with the decline of organized religious practice and the simultaneous shift in self-identification, with more and more Americans classifying themselves as spiritual but not religious, traditional faith communities have moved from the center to the margins of American culture in terms of their influence on our meaning making. What about 12-step groups such as Alcoholics Anonymous? A significant number of Americans attend 12-step meetings, and for many it is an important part of their spirituality. As a pastoral counselor and mental health practitioner, I have referred many clients struggling with one form of addiction or another to 12-step groups because I believe in the basic philosophy of confessing our powerlessness and subsequently turning our lives over to a Higher Power as we as individuals understand that Higher Power to be. Twelve-step is an important part of the recovery and treatment process for addiction, yet, as vital as it is, it is not the context for in-depth reflection about core theological beliefs. Nor is the family, the bedrock of American society. True, more than a few families consider themselves to be not only spiritual but also religious. Still, with life getting busier, with parents becoming more skillful at multitasking, and with children's schedules filling up with one activity after another, the American family, no matter how well intentioned, often lacks the time and the focus to be at the heart of substantive meaning making in this culture. That leaves the media, who are more than willing to step in and fill the void through the bombardment of news coverage, commentary, and analysis. And yet, "exposure to the media in times like these can be a double-edged sword." As the authors of *In the Wake of 9/11* pointed out, and it bears repeating:

> Much of the information presented is redundant and not of much real use in helping to make sense out of the many facets of the events with which we are struggling. Thus although some level of exposure to the news regarding terrorist attacks and other crises seems essential in facilitating coping, overexposure to the news can actually overwhelm the individual's ability to cope and can lead to exaggerated feelings of fear and hopelessness. (Pyszczynski et al., 2003, p. 136)

So much for the news media's taking up the slack and suddenly becoming the new purveyor of meaning and understanding. All of which leaves us where? Back to therapy and counseling as the unique setting or place for ascertaining whether the core theological beliefs of a client, central to the way that he or she gives meaning to the world, have the capacity to calm the person's fears or, in certain cases, make them worse. For psychotherapy to be effective in treating the new anxiety, it must take seriously "the determining and transforming activity of spirit in the self-conscious subject" to "accurately reflect what grounds and generates the quality of man's [sic] becoming." What grounds and generates the quality of our becoming are core theological beliefs, the basis for how we view the world and make sense of it. The theologian Paul Tillich, writing in another age of anxiety, once commented that "psychotherapy cannot remove ontological anxiety, because it cannot change the structure of finitude. But it can remove compulsory forms of anxiety and can reduce the frequency and intensity of fears. It can put anxiety in its proper place" (as quoted in Kierkegaard, 1981, pp. xv–xvii).

Even with the new anxiety, psychotherapy has certain limitations. As Tillich writes, it cannot change the reality of our finitude; but this is where I challenge Tillich in saying that it can, by intentionally addressing the core theological beliefs of clients and by helping to guide them in the development of a meaningful theological framework with which to interpret the present and future and, in so doing, even put ontological anxiety or an anxiety stemming from the overinvestment of meaning in its proper place. This presupposes a willingness on the part of therapists and counselors when treating the new anxiety to "go there" with clients into the realm of theological and spiritual concerns, given that the type of meaning that people are seeking today is often "spiritual."

> We may thus conclude that it should not be too difficult for therapists to accommodate for spiritual concerns in their own therapeutic work—that is if they believe it is important to do so and if they want to do so. (Schreurs, 2002, p. 201)

The urgent need for practitioners to accommodate for spiritual and theological concerns in their therapy and counseling, to "go there" even if a client does not, is illustrated by the more superficial forms of meaning making related to the events of September 11:

> For many Americans, the events of 9/11 have strengthened their view of America as entirely good and America's enemies as purely evil. But whether the explanations offered are simple or complex, false or accurate, for some people, they have failed to provide the type of understanding and meaning that is craved. Beyond pragmatic or political explanations, most people also need a deeper cosmic meaning, a general sense of how these events fit into the larger scheme of things, perhaps an understanding that finds some good in the horrible events. [Ernest] Becker referred to this sort of meaning as sacred. Such meaning is often frankly religious or spiritual in nature and entails a conception of how we fit into an order of things that stretches beyond what we can observe. (Pyszczynski et al., 2003, p. 138)

The Case of Beth

At this point, after developing a theoretical rationale for why practitioners must be intentional when it comes to addressing the core theological beliefs of anxious clients, the question becomes, how? How do we, as psychotherapists, mental health practitioners, and even pastoral counselors, help our clients discover a deeper, cosmic meaning that is theological or spiritual, one that provides a framework for situating the momentous events of the present and future? How do we—even if we have no degree in religious or theological studies, let alone a credential as an ordained member of the clergy—take the initiative to engage the client in terms of his or her religious or theological concerns? The question, in a supermodern post–September 11 world, is not unimportant, nor is it one among many others in the context of therapy and counseling. It could very well be the central question when it comes to the treatment of the new anxiety. We could, for example, sidestep the whole conversation, much like the therapist in the clinical training videotape. Or, we could, conversely, follow the method of theological reflection put forward in the commentary addressing the second clinical vignette. For example, are the client's core theological beliefs part of a closed, rigid, and therefore inflexible cognitive system, or are they open to revision or change, if necessary? Can the client, through effective therapeutic interventions, see when his or her core beliefs are a resource for health and healing and when they do more harm than good? How do we help the anxious in our care revise and even change certain core theological beliefs so that their belief systems can be a source of genuine strength and sustenance in a time of great transition and uncertainty?

Beth, a 38-year-old wife and mother of two small children, made an appointment to see me for counseling several months after the tragic events of September 11, 2001. She disclosed that her best friend's brother, who had worked in the World Trade Center, was one of the victims of the terrorist attacks. In the months after September 11, Beth made it a point, even with all the other demands placed on her time, to call or see her friend on a daily basis and to be the mainstay of the woman's support network. Recently, the visits and the telephone calls have become more infrequent as Beth's friend "begins to move on with her life." What caught Beth off guard, however, and precipitated the initial counseling appointment was, in Beth's words, "the fact that my best friend, who lost her brother, can move on with her life and I can't." Living in the southern part of Marin County, California, Beth had been anxious watching the F-16 fighter jets patrol the shores of the Bay Area, the city of San Francisco, and one of the most famous landmarks in America, the Golden Gate Bridge. She was worrying more and more as she watched and listened to the news commentators and analysts on the television warn San Franciscans that there was a good chance that they could be the next target of terrorist activity. Nor did it help her anxiety any when she accompanied her family on outings to the Golden Gate National Recreation Area for what she hoped would be a day of rest and relaxation, only to see, again and again, a rather visible show of force by police and the National Guard. Beth's apprehensive expectation of terrorist attacks in the Bay Area, her deep concern that the world that her children will inherit will be a far more dangerous place, and the emotional impact of listening to her friend recount day after day for several months the horrors of September 11 had left her in an anxious state of chronic worry.

Interestingly enough, it was not any of these things that Beth wanted to focus on in the first few weeks of counseling. Instead, what she wanted to discuss at the outset had to do with a sermon that she had heard preached by a minister on television, titled "Why Do the Innocent Suffer?" The minister, in recounting the terrible events of September 11, had situated the tragedy into the context of a theology of theodicy. The theology of theodicy grapples with the timeless question of why there is suffering and evil in the world, in a world created by a God who, so the thinking goes, is all powerful as well as all loving. But therein is the problem. God, according to the theology of the Judeo-Christian tradition, is both omnipotent and the very essence of love. Why, then, would a loving God, who has the power to eliminate suffering and evil in the world, choose not to do so? Theologies abound that try to sort out the complexities of this bewildering conundrum. For example, there is the free will argument: God is omnipotent but because of divine love, limits the extent of that power so that human beings have the freedom to make their own decisions, good or bad. Thus, when we mistreat one another or, out of ignorance, make decisions that are harmful to other people, it is not God's doing but ours. The argument holds up when it addresses human evil but falls apart when the issue is the natural evils of God's creation—for example, earthquakes, floods, and so forth. Humans do have a role in these misfortunes, too, such as when we build houses on fault lines or in flood plains. Acknowledging this, however, does not let God off the hook entirely. Because of God's omnipotence and deep love for human beings and the whole created order, we would think that God would unambiguously want to eliminate these so-called natural evils and their potential for destruction.

Another theology of theodicy, one applied by the television preacher to the events of September 11, is the so-called soul-making approach to human suffering. Those who embrace the perspective of soul making believe that everything happens for a reason and that suffering, misfortune, and even terrible tragedies like September 11 come to us by way of the hand of God. Why would this be the case, if God is all loving? The reason, according to this theological view, is that God puts us through the fires of trial and tribulation for our own good, to see what we are made of and to test the depths of our faith. We suffer because God wants us to suffer. Suffering is therefore a part of the divine plan for human beings, the quintessential character builder. Beth, as she listened to this on the television, was startled by the intensity of her emotional reaction, as was her husband, who was listening to the sermon with her. She explained that on hearing the television preacher say, "Every problem and hardship and tragedy is a character-building opportunity sent to us from God" and "The greater the degree of difficulty and pain, the greater the potential for building spiritual muscle," she experienced an intense visceral reaction. Beth recounted that as she listened to this part of the sermon, her thoughts turned to the events of September 11, to her friend who lost her brother as the Twin Towers collapsed, and to her two small children, who are growing up in a dangerous world. As these thoughts came to mind, Beth instinctively exclaimed, "What the hell! No! That's not right!" Embarrassed, she immediately apologized to her husband, who was looking at her dumbfounded. He encouraged her to "find someone to talk to," which prompted her to schedule an appointment with me for counseling:

> KB: Welcome, Beth. You sounded anxious on the phone yesterday.
> BETH: I know I need to talk to someone.
> KB: About . . .
> BETH: About everything. Why the world's going to hell, why there doesn't seem to be a future, why there's so much pain and suffering.
> KB: Can you be more specific?
> BETH: My best friend's brother was in the World Trade Center on September 11. A handsome young guy with his whole life ahead of him. My God, how his sister has suffered.
> KB: What about you? Have you suffered?
> BETH: I feel ashamed coming here today to talk about me.
> KB: Because?
> BETH: What do I have to complain about? I live in one of the greatest places in the world. I have a great marriage. My family's healthy. My best friend— now, she has a right to complain.
> KB: Maybe so. At the same time, what brings *you* here today?
> BETH: I can't stop worrying.
> KB: About?

BETH: About everything.

KB: Can you close your eyes for a minute?

BETH: Okay.

KB: When you hear me ask, "What are you most worried about?" what immediately comes to mind?

BETH: My kids. I worry for them. The world's not a safe place anymore. The fighter jets go overhead every day. We see the [National] Guard on the [Golden Gate] bridge. I can't get it out of my mind. I'm so afraid.

KB: What brings you peace and comfort? Anything?

BETH: That's the thing. It's what brought me here.

KB: Say more.

BETH: I went online to see if there was any spiritual counseling in the area. I found you. I'm not a religious person, but I'm very spiritual. I've had therapists before who don't even want to discuss it with me.

KB: Don't want to discuss what with you?

BETH: You know, my spirituality.

KB: Is that something that brings you comfort?

BETH: I thought it did, but now I don't know. I just want to have someplace where I can go to talk about this.

KB: What about your husband?

BETH: He'd rather not talk about it. My emotions scare him away.

KB: You mentioned that you're a spiritual person but not a religious person. Do you belong to any faith community? Any minister you can talk to?

BETH: No. I thought about getting my kids involved in a church. But to be honest—and no offense—religion scares me. All that dogma and doctrine. Everyone has to believe all the same things. It's almost like a form of mind control. I want my kids to have the freedom to believe whatever they want to believe.

KB: What about you, Beth? What do you believe?

BETH: What do you mean?

KB: What do you believe about the world, September 11, God?

BETH: That's really what I want to talk about today.

KB: Go ahead.

BETH: The other night my husband and I were sitting in the living room watching TV. He was channel surfing and came upon this TV preacher who was preaching on why we suffer.

KB: What did the preacher say?

BETH: He said that everything happens for a reason, even tragedies like September 11. It's supposed to make us stronger.

KB: How do you feel about that?

BETH: When he said that, the image of my best friend and her brother flashed through my mind and all the other victims and those they left behind. What's the point? What's the lesson we're supposed to learn from a terrorist attack?

KB: It sounds like what the preacher said triggered something very powerful in you.

BETH: It caught my husband so off guard. That's why he suggested I call you.

KB: What got triggered?

BETH: I couldn't accept that a good and loving God would make airplanes fly into buildings and kill people. That's what made me stand up and shout "No!"

KB: Who or what were you saying no to?

BETH: I don't know, probably the minister, religion, the terrorists.

KB: Anyone or anything else?

BETH: Yes, now that you ask [extended pause].

KB: Go on . . .

BETH: God. But I don't believe God made September 11 happen just to teach us a lesson. What could possibly be the lesson?

KB: I agree, Beth. That doesn't square with my theology of God either.

BETH: But then I get scared and anxious. What's the alternative? A world without God? A world where everything that happens is just random?

KB: How would you answer your own questions?

BETH: I struggle with it. The minister talked about theodicy: God is love, God is power, but we still suffer. I suppose we just have to accept it.

KB: Accept what?

BETH: That God causes these things for our own good so that we can grow and develop. You know, God is all powerful, so everything happens for a reason, even September 11.

KB: Just pause for a minute, Beth. As you listen to yourself, do you honestly believe what you just said?

BETH: No, I don't know, I mean, what's the alternative? If God isn't omnipotent and involved in the world, then my kids grow up in a world of randomness. I think that's what I worry about the most.

KB: Sounds like you're between the proverbial rock and a hard place: Either God is involved in the world and makes airplanes crash into populated buildings, or we're all alone.

BETH: As you said that, I got a knot in my stomach.

KB: What do you mean?

BETH: It triggered my fear and anxiety.

KB: About what?

BETH: My kids being alone in a world where there's no point.

KB: Can I propose a third alternative?

BETH: Sure.

KB: Right now, there are only two: Either God is with us, even if God is complicit with bad things happening to us, or we're all alone. What if those aren't the only two possibilities?

BETH: I don't like either one. But they're all we have.

KB: Not necessarily.

BETH: What else could there be? The thought of my kids growing up in a world of randomness really scares me.

KB: What about the thought of them growing up in a world where God may decide at any moment to put them through the ringer, just to see what they're made of? Is that any better?

BETH: Actually it's worse.

KB: So, let's try on for size a third possibility. That sound okay?

BETH: I'm listening.

KB: My own personal belief is that we are not alone, that God is with us. It's just a matter of what that means and what that looks like.

BETH: I agree.

KB: What if God is more love and presence than power?

BETH: So, God isn't omnipotent? What good is God?

KB: Some believe that God is intimately involved in the world, just not in the traditional sense. The events of September 11, for example, the Holocaust, and many others force us to reassess the traditional view of God being omnipotent.

BETH: Then what is God?

KB: Again, for some, God is that loving presence that we feel during and after times of crisis, manifested in the care and support we receive from friends, family, and the local community.

BETH: After September 11, I began reading Rabbi Kushner's book *When Bad Things Happen to Good People*. Never read it before. His son died tragically. He talks about having to let go of the image of an all-powerful God and accept that God is more of a loving presence, like you're saying.

KB: How do you feel when reading the book or hearing yourself recount it now?

BETH: I know he's right.

KB: Right about what?

BETH: Right about God being a loving presence. Right about having to let go of God as omnipotent.

KB: It sounds like you're already familiar with the third option. My hunch is that you're familiar with it and now just need to try it on for size. How does that sound?

BETH: Scary.

KB: What scares you?

BETH: Having to let go of the image of God as powerful.

KB: What if God's power is the power of love, not the power of might?

BETH: Never thought of it that way.

KB: Can you close your eyes again?

BETH: Sure.

KB: Think of a time when you have felt very anxious. Can you picture it in your mind?

BETH: Yes.

KB: Can you feel the emotions of that moment?

BETH: Yes, definitely.

KB: What are you feeling?

BETH: I feel tense and anxious.

KB: What's making you feel tense and anxious?

BETH: I'm sitting in the backyard with my best friend. She's recounting the last few minutes of her brother's life. I watch my children playing together on the swing set. And there they come, those damn fighter jets, out of nowhere. I get this knot in my stomach.

KB: And where is God?

BETH: I don't know. Does it even matter?

KB: Yes, Beth, I believe that it does matter. And you know what I think? I think you believe it matters, too.

BETH: I wish I knew. All this craziness. The world's going to hell and God doesn't care.

KB: How do you know that?

BETH: Because God's omnipotent, you know, all powerful. He could intervene and do something if he wanted to.

KB: Maybe God does intervene, just not the way we expect.

BETH: What do you mean?

KB: Back to what we discussed earlier: What if God intervenes not with brute power and force but with love and care and tenderness? What if God is there in the backyard with you and your friend and your children to love and support and sustain you? [Beth nods her head forward and begins to cry.] What's happening, Beth?

BETH: I have to let go of the worry. It's killing me.

KB: Yes. What are you feeling?

BETH: Relief. Peace. It will be okay. It really will. God loves us.

KB: God does love us. And God is there, with loving arms around you and your friend and your precious children when those fighter jets fly overhead.

BETH: I know, I know [crying]. It's accepting God for who he is, not who I want him to be. It's hard.

KB: I know it is.

BETH: But I can't live with a knot in my stomach anymore.

KB: No, Beth, you can't.

BETH: I'm feeling a little more relaxed.

KB: That's a good thing. It's important to track yourself and notice what you're feeling.

BETH: It feels like the tension is leaving my stomach and body [sits back for the first time in the session and exhales].

The case vignette with Beth illustrates, rather vividly, the application of CBT to the treatment of the new anxiety. Recall that CBT focuses on the core beliefs of the client and how these foundational beliefs affect, for better or worse, the way that the client views and makes sense of her or his life and the surrounding world. For Beth, even though she, like many Americans, does not consider herself to be religious per se (she is spiritual, not religious), the core organizing belief that is central to her meaning making is clearly theological. She struggles with God's role in and involvement with the world, particularly as she reflects on her children growing up in a world where terrorists fly airplanes into buildings, where F-16 fighter jets fly directly overhead, where ordinary citizens are under heightened surveillance on bridges, in parks, at airports, and so on. The fact that she has been a significant caregiver to her friend over the course of several months, that she has heard recounted again and again the tragic and horrific circumstances of September 11, leaves her feeling anxious. We could say that because of her symptoms, Beth presents with the new anxiety. If we refer back to the diagnostic criteria established in the previous chapter, we see that Beth has more than a few of the characteristic features:

A. Excessive anxiety and worry (apprehensive expectation) about a number of potentially significant issues and events.
B. Difficulty controlling or containing the worry.
C. The anxiety and worry are associated (for Beth) with the following symptoms: restlessness or feeling keyed up or on edge, being easily fatigued (after overextending herself caring for her friend), irritability (the flash of rage directed at the television preacher), muscle tension (the "knot in my stomach").
D. The anxiety is proportional to the impact of and subsequent fallout from feared events (the fighter jets overhead are a daily reminder that even though San Francisco is on the West Coast, 3,000 miles away from Ground Zero in New York City, the Bay Area is just as vulnerable to a terrorist attack).
E. The anxiety is exacerbated not by the collapse or loss of meaning, as postmodernism sees it, but by the intense need to give meaning to a rapidly changing world (we could say that in a sense, Beth is intensely trying to apply a traditional category of meaning, such as divine omnipotence, to a supermodern post–September 11 world that requires new theological categories).
F. The proliferation of nonplaces is an obstacle that thwarts our attempts at finding new meaning, thus making someone like Beth feel even more anxious (the downside of being spiritual but not religious is that Beth has removed herself from traditional contexts of meaning making—although, as we have just seen, therapy or counseling has the

potential for becoming the relational place where she discovers new meaning).

It was, to be sure, Beth's core theological belief about the nature of God and God's particular mode of involvement in the world that was fueling her anxiety. From a cognitive standpoint, anytime that she saw the fighter jets soar overhead and the simultaneous look of confusion and bewilderment on the faces of her children; anytime she listened to her friend recount the terrible events of September 11, especially, the tragic loss of her beloved brother; anytime she heard, as in the case of the television preacher, that God had a purpose in either causing September 11 or at the very least allowing the terrorist attacks to occur, Beth would immediately gravitate toward the core theological belief in God's omnipotence. Put simply, the belief could be summed up in the words of the old song "He's Got the Whole World in His Hands." But she was not feeling as if God has the whole world in his hands at this particular moment; or if God was still in control, then in certain ways, this created for her a more difficult, if not disturbing, theological problem. All of which brought Beth full circle, back to the issue of theodicy: God is all powerful; God is all loving; there is no shortage of pain and suffering and evil in the world. This was the focus of the television preacher's sermon, not that it provided Beth with any hope, comfort, or peace. The preacher embraced a soul-making solution to the theodicy problem: Tragedy, hardship, and misfortune come from an all-powerful and, paradoxically, an all-loving God who wants to toughen us up spiritually. Beth, because of the automaticity of her unexamined core beliefs, found herself agreeing with the preacher, at least initially, only to surprise herself and her husband later by reacting strongly against the theology that she thought she embraced. What she did not know and what would come to light in the course of the counseling was that the core theological belief of God's omnipotence, which she clung to tenaciously, was doing her more harm than good. Put another way, Beth's core belief in the omnipotence of God, rather than quelling her anxiety, was actually making her anxiety much worse.

None of this would have surfaced in the treatment had I applied a conventional psychoanalytic framework to Beth's presenting issues. If that had been the case, I would have, much as the therapist did in the training videotape, steered her away from any theological talk about God. For example, when she recounted the television preacher's sermon on God, theodicy, and the tragedy of September 11, when she herself intimated, "I don't believe God made September 11 happen just to teach us a lesson," I would have intervened with something like "Okay, that's what you think God would or wouldn't do. More important, I want to know what *you* are going to do, how *you* are going to respond to the aftermath of September 11." In so doing, I would have, for all intents, managed to close the door on Beth's core theological beliefs or, at the very least, make her feel so inhibited that she would close the door on them herself in deference to me, the "expert." What I would have missed was the fundamental link between her uncontrollable worry and apprehensive expectation and her core theological belief that God is all powerful. True, there would have been plenty of other important issues for us to discuss, such as her relationship with her husband, the demands of parenting two small children in frightening and uncertain times, the demands of being the primary caregiver for a grieving friend, and so forth. All very important issues, but none was central to the issue of her anxiety. What was central to the issue of her anxiety, what was fueling her apprehensive expectation about the present and the future, was the core theological belief in the omnipotence of God. With the automaticity of her thinking, Beth had no idea that the core belief that God was in total perfect control of the world was exacerbating her anxiety. This would have remained underground if Beth and I had not "gone there" into the realm of her core theological beliefs. The fact is that core beliefs do frequently remain underground in the context of contemporary psychotherapy and mental health counseling.

It does not have to be this way, nor should it be this way, especially when we are talking about the treatment of the new anxiety. Again, I could have steered Beth away from any discussion having to do with religion, theology, and spirituality, as more than a few practitioners would have opted to do. This, however, as we can see from the case study, would have been most unfortunate because, as Schreurs (2002) points out so convincingly, it would have compelled Beth to split off her spirituality and core theological beliefs and thereby lose a vital lifeline to the Transcendent. It is true that her current beliefs about the Transcendent or God were actually fueling her anxiety, which would certainly prompt some practitioners, seemingly in the spirit of Freud, to convey either directly or indirectly that it is in her best interests to abandon her core beliefs about God and the nature of God's involvement in the world and grow up into reality. By doing so, according to the traditional psychoanalytic view, Beth would avoid remaining a child forever, emotionally and developmentally. Yet, other psychoanalysts, most notably, Ana-Maria Rizzuto (1979), who has done extensive research on images or representations of God in the human psyche, has clearly demonstrated that although our beliefs in God may indeed at times stunt our growth and development, they can at other times be a vital resource for growth and healing. Therapeutic neutrality, then, toward a client's core theological beliefs is in order at the outset of the treatment until a determination can be made as to whether they calm or fuel a client's worry and apprehensive expectation. Then and only then, through abundant amounts of empathic understanding, will we be able to assess the impact of those beliefs on the person's psychological health and well-being. With Beth, it was only after hearing her out and allowing her to "go there," into the realm of her core beliefs about God, God's involvement in our lives, and the present and future state of the world, that I was able to see the double-edgedness of her theology. On one hand, her core theological belief about God's omnipotence was reinforcing her anxiety, yet on the other, revising, changing, or updating her foundational belief about the nature of God gave her a measure of genuine comfort and peace.

When it comes to treating the new anxiety, psychotherapists, mental health practitioners, and pastoral counselors misstep when they avoid, gloss over, or ignore the core theological beliefs of anxious clients. In an age of supermodernity characterized by the urgent need to find meaning in and give meaning to an overabundance of national and world events at precisely the same moment when there are fewer and fewer places to do so, therapy or counseling becomes, out of necessity, the place for exploring one's core beliefs about God, God's role in the world and in our lives, and our role as co-creators with God. The anxiety that Beth was experiencing was fundamentally connected to these core theological beliefs; thus, to have avoided them or ignored them would have been tantamount to avoiding the basis of her anxiety. Moreover, it would have ignored the method put forward by Schreurs for, in the words of the subtitle of her important book, "integrating the spiritual dimension into therapeutic practice." The time has come, I argue, for practitioners to integrate the spiritual dimension into therapeutic practice in general and, even more so, into the treatment of the new anxiety. In fact, in a supermodern post–September 11 world characterized by no shortage of anxiety about the present and the future, combined with the accelerated pace of life that mitigates against finding new meaning in current events, therapy becomes the place where anxious clients can go to explore the relation of their core theological beliefs to their present levels of worry and apprehensive expectation. This again highlights for practitioners the vital lifeline that core beliefs are to God or to the Transcendent, becoming a valuable resource in the treatment of the new anxiety. As Philip Sheldrake writes in the preface to Nuth's *God's Lovers in an Age of Anxiety* (2001),

> Nowadays, in the Western world, there is a widespread hunger for spirituality in all its forms. This is not confined to traditional religious people let alone to regular churchgoers. The desire for resources to sustain the spiritual quest has led many people to seek wisdom in unfamiliar places. (p. 7)

The "unfamiliar place" for seeking wisdom or meaning in the new age of anxiety has become, out of necessity, the therapy or counseling session.

The anxiety that my client Beth was experiencing was fueled by her core theological beliefs in the nature of God and God's supposed role in the world, and to have avoided or ignored these core beliefs would have taken the therapy in a direction away from the fundamental roots of her anxiety. When she heard the television preacher put forward the idea that God was still very much in control of the world, that he has the whole world in his hands despite the terrible events of September 11, the automaticity of her response was such that she ended up agreeing with the preacher's theology even though another part of her wanted to say, and did in fact say, "No!" But to abandon the core belief of divine omnipotence, even though that belief comes at a rather steep price—namely, having to affirm that tragedies like September 11 are supposedly God's way of putting us to the test to build spiritual and moral character—was simply too unsettling for Beth. One part of her, the part that refuses to accept any theology that rationalizes away the tragic and untimely deaths of thousands of people simply to keep God looking strong, mighty, and invincible—that is, omnipotent—stepped forward to utter a resounding "No!" Another part of her, however, became anxious and fearful with the possibility that in saying "No!" she was also saying no to God's omnipotence and any hope of divine control in our world. Yet, what Beth did not understand was that in clinging tenaciously to her belief that God was powerfully in control, even though this means at times subjecting ourselves to the severity of God's discipline, her anxiety was getting worse, not better. She was, as Schreurs points out in the case study of the 40-year-old woman who lost her child in a car accident, trapped in a closed cognitive system where if core beliefs are left unexamined, there can be no other role for God than the leading role in linking causes to their seeming linear effects. Beth's search for a harmonious relationship with God was and is, in my professional estimation, something favorable for therapeutic and spiritual growth. It was not, then, her relationship with God that was the problem. Rather, because we intentionally took the time to explore in depth her core theological beliefs, we could determine that it was the inflexibility of her belief about God's omnipotence that was making her feel anxious. What Beth never realized, in the context of a closed belief system, was that God could remain powerfully involved in the world, just not in the way that she imagined. The visceral response from Beth, as she exchanged a God of power and might for a God of presence and love, demonstrated that she had begun to free herself from a rigidly closed cognitive system.

I would never have discovered this, however, without probing Beth's core theological views. In fact, I was simply applying the cognitive–behavioral method put forward by McMullin in *The New Handbook of Cognitive Therapy Techniques*. Recall that McMullin's method is a five-step approach focusing on the client's core beliefs, whatever they happen to be. Moreover, as Mc-Mullin argues, CBT is effective only if the therapist or counselor is working on the correct core beliefs of the anxious client. Some practitioners would have avoided Beth's theology altogether, but in doing so, they would have missed the core belief that was triggering and reinforcing her anxiety. Following McMullin's method, I began by inviting Beth to close her eyes and relax. This was the point of transition from concentrating on certain external events to focusing more on internal processes. Second, I asked her to imagine as clearly as possible the situation that most concerns her. Beth responded by vividly recalling the events associated with September 11: the tragic loss of her best friend's brother in the World Trade Center, the eerie sound of the F-16 fighter jets roaring overhead and the subsequent look of fear and bewilderment on the faces of her children, and the military presence on the picturesque Golden Gate Bridge and inside the Golden Gate National Recreation Area. Third, while Beth had these images in her mind, I asked her to pay attention to what she was feeling. The images triggered feelings of fear, worry, and apprehensive expectation. In terms of McMullin's method, Beth and I began with the A, the situation and the real or perceived events that she was most concerned about. Then, with the A in mind, she noticed the C, what she was feeling: fear, worry, and apprehension about the present and the future. Fourth, we then turned our attention to Beth's thoughts, what she was telling herself about the A that was making her feel the emotion of C. What emerged was the television preacher's theology, which she, for the most part, subscribed to. In fact, we could say that the C, the anxiety that Beth was feeling, was something of a double-whammy emotional response to her beliefs, the B, about the aftermath of September 11, the A part of this equation. For example, the minister's theology, suggesting that God not only allows but even causes terrible events to occur simply to keep us morally and spiritually honest, triggered an initial feeling of anxiety in Beth that was manifested in her defiant "No!"

The theology of God's being all powerful, in absolute control of the world, brought Beth for many years of her life a significant measure of peace and comfort. But now, hearing it linked with a certain soul-making or character-developing theological perspective elicited a very different internal response, a response of utter defiance at the thought of divine power linked with so much death and destruction. In her defiance, however, Beth immediately felt anxious again, this time because in saying "No!" to an all-powerful God who subjects us to horrific events just to see what we are made of, she was on the verge of affirming a world where God's involvement is, at most, rather am-biguous. And looking into the faces of her frightened children, not to men-tion noticing the fear that this potential theological shift had evoked in her, she had no alternative, or so she thought, but to return to the confines of a familiar belief system. Beth was, so to speak, in something of a catch-22: ei-ther let go of the core belief affirming God's omnipotence, which when com-bined with the view of soul making was making her feel particularly anxious, or cling to this core theological belief in an attempt to quell the anxiety, which at best gave her a temporary feeling of relief but in the long run left her feeling even more anxious. Beth could not feel secure living in a world where there is no God or, more to the point, a world devoid of God's in-volvement. This core theological belief was therefore hardly a peripheral matter in the treatment. Rather, it connected her to the ground of her being, becoming, as it were, a vital lifeline to the Transcendent.

We would never have gotten to this point, the foundation of Beth's belief system in times of crisis, without a willingness to probe the depths of her the-ology. Nor would the therapy or counseling have had the capacity to put her anxiety in its place. In line with McMullin's method, however, we moved to the fifth step where, because of interventions aimed directly at Beth's core theological beliefs, we were able to get to the bottom of her anxiety and do something about it. As McMullin suggests, the practitioner keeps the A in mind, the belief in divine omnipotence, and begins to ask certain questions in an attempt to get at even more basic and fundamental beliefs. McMullin points out that it is important to keep asking questions and to even offer "what if?" scenarios. Along the way, we listen carefully to the answers that clients give us, waiting for their imagination to originate a thought that will point us in the direction of a core belief. Beth, within the confines of a closed cognitive system, had decided that there were only two alternatives when it came to God's involvement in the world: Either God is with us, even if God, ostensibly for our own good, makes bad things happen to good people, or we are all alone in a world of randomness. Simple questions that I put to her, such as "Can I propose a third alternative?" "What if these aren't the only two possibilities?" and "What if God is more love and presence than power?" prompted Beth to think outside the box of conventional theological beliefs and consider alternatives. As a result, we managed to access her core theo-logical belief in the omnipotence of God, which functioned as a sort of pro-tective shield against the fear that her children (and she herself) were living in a world of randomness, where the tragedy of September 11 has absolutely no rhyme or reason. But there was a third possibility, which Beth had not considered, or if she had considered it, she was, at least up until now, holding it at arm's length (recall that she had familiarized herself with Rabbi Kushner's theology of divine presence). Beth had begun to revise her core theological belief about the nature of God and God's involvement in the world and, in doing so, was experiencing less anxiety. The intervention of a third alternative, namely, God's involvement in the world manifested in love and presence rather than in might and force, was, so to speak, a pressure-release valve that gave Beth the opportunity to make needed changes to her core beliefs while remaining tethered to the vital lifeline of God or the Transcendent.

From this case vignette, we can see that Beth is a rather motivated client. Thus, we were able in this counseling session to access her core theological and ontological beliefs about life, the present and future states of the world, and the nature of God and God's involvement in the world. For other clients, however, those who are less open and more guarded and defended, the core belief may not surface in the first session or even in the second or third. In these cases, it is important to remember, as McMullin (2000) suggests, that when trying to change beliefs, it is usually best not to work on the core belief first. It is, for the defended client, too far away from his or her immediate awareness and is therefore often not acknowledged. Cognitive therapists usually work from the surface downward, tackling core beliefs after the client has shown some skill with surface thoughts. The process described by Mc-Mullin is illustrated, practically in toto, in the case vignette with Beth. Mc-Mullin's method, of course, must be tailored to the particularities of the treatment with any given anxious client. Still, whatever the pace of the treatment, the goal in working with the new anxiety is to get to the core beliefs and, in many cases, the core theological beliefs of anxious individuals, remembering all the while that it is not so much life events that make people anxious as it is what they believe about these events. McMullin puts it this way:

> Events are not critical because of what happened to clients but rather because of what they *concluded* about what happened. They may recover from a traumatic event like the death of their grandmother if they conclude that Grandma had a full, rich life and is living with God in heaven. But they may never get over the death of their pet goldfish if they conclude that God shouldn't let goldfish die since he didn't create a goldfish heaven for them to go to.

It's not the strength of the experience that makes the event critical; it's the brute force of the client's conclusions. Clients' deductions about tiny things can be enormous. It's as if they are walking down one path in life when they trip over a pebble and suddenly turn down a totally different road. These conclusions become life themes that serve as road maps guiding them through life. (pp. 80–81)

~

CHAPTER FIVE

Maintaining a Balanced Approach

This we can all bear witness to, living as we do plagued by unremitting anxiety. It becomes more and more imperative that the life of the spirit be avowed as the only firm basis upon which to establish happiness and peace.

—The Dalai Lama

In the previous chapter, I discuss the importance of focusing on the core theological beliefs of anxious clients. In an age of great change, fear mongering, and difficulty finding meaning in the overabundance of world and national events, therapy or counseling, to be effective, must take seriously the religious or spiritual dimension of human experience. We saw in the vignette from the training videotape what occurs when core theological beliefs are not taken seriously. Although this was not a client who was presenting the new anxiety, she was nonetheless anxious about her deceased son's status in the afterlife and whether God could be trusted to care for the boy. The therapist was certainly effective in treating the client's grief and depression, yet intentionally or unintentionally, he avoided her theology and therefore missed a valuable opportunity to address her anxious feelings. Think if this had been someone like Beth, a client who did present with the new anxiety. To have avoided her core theological beliefs would have meant, from a therapeutic and intervention standpoint, missing the mark completely. With the second vignette, the case of the unfaithful wife who believed that the death of her young child was punishment for her sinful actions, we witnessed a very different approach to the client's core theological beliefs. Here, the theology of the client was taken more seriously and treated more respectfully. The latter approach gave us a method for reflecting, theologically, on the core religious or spiritual beliefs of a client, something that is fundamental to the treatment of the new anxiety. Clearly, in an age where people struggle to keep up as best they can with the accelerated pace of life, struggle to find places where they can try to make sense of a world in transition, the task of meaning making becomes fundamental to the work of caring for the anxious.

The case vignette with Beth illustrates the necessity of addressing the core theological beliefs of anxious clients. If I had merely applied a cognitive–behavioral framework without taking into consideration the spiritual dimension of Beth's experience, then the focus of the treatment would have been on Beth's thinking about, for example, the terrible events of September 11, the tragic death of her friend's brother, her friend's grief, and raising children in a post–September 11 world. Not that her thinking about these particular issues is unimportant. On the contrary, it is very important. And yet, to address her thinking about these issues apart from her core theological beliefs about the nature of God, God's role in the world, and our role as co-creators with God would have led to a situation where, as Schreurs (2002) warned, the spiritual is in danger of being split off. For some, perhaps, more than a few practitioners, this would not be a problem, because Beth's theology is quite clearly the source of her anxiety. At the same time, however, practitioners, by ignoring, avoiding, or even dismissing her theology, would fail to see that it is a resource for authentic hope and healing, as well as a vital lifeline to God or the Transcendent. As we can see from the case vignette with Beth, I purposely interjected some of my own personal theology as a point of contrast and comparison. I was not imposing my belief system onto her, nor was I attempting to convert her to my way of thinking. What I did was offer her a way of reframing the situation, of revising her core belief in God from an omnipotent force of power and might to a force of love and presence. This intervention had the immediate effect of reducing her level of anxiety while keeping her connected to the Transcendent, albeit in a different way.

The Urgent Need for New Paradigms

Some therapists and counselors will have difficulty thinking outside the box of conventional psychotherapeutic paradigms and making room in the counseling session for the core theological beliefs of anxious clients. Even more difficult, at least for some practitioners, will be keeping an open mind about bringing the caregiver's theological views into the treatment. Most of us have been trained to be therapeutically neutral or, at least, to think that we can practice in this manner. But as the stance of neutral and objective scientific inquiry has been rigorously critiqued in recent years, so, too, has the stance of value-neutral psychotherapy. No human being can be completely objective, no matter how scientific one thinks himself or herself to be. The scientist approaches the object of study, whatever it may be, with a certain set of assumptions and questions. This becomes, as it were, the lens through which the object of study is viewed or observed. Questions that we can ask the scientific observer might include the following: Why do you approach the problem, the issue, or the situation with this set of assumptions? Why not another set of assumptions that other scientists would consider to be more helpful? Why ask these questions and not others? How do you determine what questions to ask and what questions not to ask? How do you make this decision? What personal values and presuppositions motivate you to look at the object of study this way and not another way? And so on and so on. We begin to see, without any difficulty, the elusiveness of neutrality and objectivity in any given field of study. These particular constructs may be true in theory, but in practice, they simply do not hold up under scrutiny. This is not necessarily a bad thing. In fact, there is no need to attach any value judgment, good or bad, to the reality of there being no perfect neutrality or objectivity in the world of human affairs. This is simply the way it is.

This applies to the fields of psychotherapy, mental health counseling, and pastoral counseling. No longer can practitioners go about their work all the while assuming that they are being neutral and objective. Therapists and counselors, as I point out in chapter 1, have been forced to acknowledge that if basic scientific research cannot be value-free, then neither can an applied discipline such as psychotherapy. Nor, I argue, should we ever want psychotherapy to be a neutral enterprise in the first place. I am all for client-centered therapy, but with all due respect to Carl Rogers, sometimes we must intervene and let clients know that certain beliefs and values relative to self, others, and God increase rather than decrease their levels of anxiety. Moreover, as practitioners working in the field of mental health care, we are morally obligated to inform our clients where we stand on issues relevant to the treatment. This does not mean that we are overstepping appropriate boundaries, as would be the case with role reversal. I am not suggesting that we lecture clients or educate them about the merits of our belief systems or have them listen to us at length as if they are there to care for us. What I am saying is that we are not treating the new anxiety effectively if we steadfastly refuse to share anything about ourselves with anxious clients. Think about it: Imagine a client who is presenting with the new anxiety, apprehensive about the present state of the nation and world, unsure of whether God has the whole world in his hands or not, uncertain about the meaning or purpose of life in a post–September 11 world, wondering if the future is simply a crap-shoot or if it is more than that. What if that client asks you or me, in a state of high anxiety, "What do you believe?" We could, so to speak, play a game of dodgeball, supposedly because we are committed to therapeutic neutrality, responding to the anxious client in a sort of Rogerian way: "That's a very interesting question. What makes *you* ask it?" or "What do *you* believe about it?" or à la the therapist in the training videotape, "I want to know what *you* would say." To be quite honest, I cannot think of a more ineffective approach with an anxious client than one that is modeled on the premise of value neutrality. If the client is someone who is presenting the new anxiety, if he or she is someone intent on making greater sense of a world in transition, value-neutral therapy will have the undesired effect of making him or her even more anxious. I am well aware that

> there are divergent opinions in the mental health field regarding how to manage clients' curiosity about counselors' personal beliefs. Most psychoanalytic therapists hold that such self-disclosure inhibits clients' autonomy and their opportunity to freely explore their feelings and beliefs especially in arenas that are morally sensitive.

The power differential, to be sure, between therapist and client is real and must be handled with great care and sensitivity. We need only remember what transpired in the vignette from the training videotape when the therapist intervened by telling the client that he was more interested in her perspective than God's. She immediately followed his leading, possibly because he is the supposed expert and she is the one in need of urgent care. Maybe the client becomes a pleaser when she interacts with an authority figure. In any case, she ended up backing down in response to his intervention, never to return to her core beliefs, at least not in this counseling session. If in fact she is a pleaser and typically defers to her therapist, think what might have happened if he had disclosed his own beliefs about the existence of God and an afterlife and whether God can be trusted to care for the boy in the world to come. Given this therapeutic relationship, there certainly would be the potential for this client, in response to the disclosure of the therapist's personal beliefs, to become overdependent, passive, and inhibited in terms of her own core beliefs. Thus, there is plenty of justification for being concerned about self-disclosure on the part of therapists, particularly when it comes to the sharing of personal values. I have more to say about this shortly. For now, it is important to keep in mind that nonreligious clients or those who have disaffiliated with their religious or spiritual traditions might worry that counselors may be judgmental about their atypical views or their departure from orthodox beliefs. Others might be concerned that atheist counselors might not provide them with an opportunity to explore alternative religions or spiritualities. . . . Still others could fear that counselors who are religious might try to convert them or to encourage in them values that are similar to their own. (Frame, 2003, p. 159)

That being said, "other counselors take an opposing view, arguing that because counseling is not value-free . . . disclosing religious and spiritual values is ethical and assists clients in maintaining autonomy." Not only that, it has the potential to assist them with the task of meaning making, a vital component in the treatment of the new anxiety. "By exposing their values, some counselors argue that clients are not subjected to inadvertent imposition of counselor values and have an opportunity to examine them critically." To disclose or not disclose one's core beliefs and values in the counseling session—that is the question for practitioners working in the context of a new age of anxiety. Other therapists and counselors hold to a middle way, deferring or deflecting questions about their personal beliefs "so that clients are led to explore the meanings implicit in such inquiries." The thinking is that "direct answers have the potential to alienate clients whose beliefs are different than those of the counselor" or, in the case of theological agreement between therapist and client, may "contribute to clients thinking they will be spared the confrontation often associated with the therapeutic process." With the latter, the theological alignment between caregiver and client, "questions regarding counselors' beliefs might mask pain and vulnerability such that a direct answer might protect clients from addressing critical concerns." The concern on the part of practitioners espousing a middle-ground strategy is that self-disclosure of core beliefs and values may encourage the client to take a flight into health or, in this case, religion and theology. Responses that defer or deflect such questions would therefore be in order:

It might be helpful to respond by saying to clients, "I value your questions, especially because it suggests something of importance to you. Rather than respond to it directly, I think it might be helpful if you were to talk a bit more about salvation (or belief in God) and how it's important to you . . ." Another possible response would be, "It sounds like you are concerned that if my beliefs are different from yours that I might try to convince you to change them and that would not be acceptable to you. Or, maybe you are worried that I won't take your religious or spiritual concerns seriously or that it isn't safe to raise these topics in counseling. I want you to know that you can trust me to respect your beliefs and to help you explore the ways in which they may be important in the work we do together." If, however, such responses elicit unrelenting questioning from clients, it is best to give a direct, honest answer than an evasion. (Frame, 2003, p. 160)

Interestingly, the middle-ground approach of deferring or deflecting a client's questions about the core personal beliefs of his or her caregiver is not all that different from the psychoanalytic view that discourages any and all self-disclosure on the part of the therapist or counselor. It does, at least on the surface, appear to be more open to and respectful of clients' questions and inquiries, which is certainly an improvement over the attitude of dismissal that we saw from the therapist in the training videotape. The anxious grieving mother in the videotape simply articulated certain theological convictions of a personal nature, without expressing any overt interest in the belief system of her caregiver. She was immediately rerouted by the therapist to issues and concerns that he thought were more important and relevant. Think if she had had the fortitude to take the discussion a step further and not back down out of deference to the "expert" and, instead, had asked him directly what he believes about God's capacity to care for a small boy in the afterlife. We can only surmise that he would have been even less interested in sharing his personal beliefs than he had been in hearing those expressed by her. A middle-ground approach to core theological beliefs would have at least motivated the therapist to express a modicum of curiosity and interest in the client's theology. Responding more thoughtfully and respectfully to her, he might have said, as was just cited, "I value your question about God because it sounds very important to you," "You can trust me to respect your beliefs and to help you explore the ways in which they may be important in the work we do together," and so forth. The client would have then felt the encouragement to explore in greater depth her core theological beliefs. From there, very possibly, because of a deeper level of trust and therapeutic rapport, she might have felt comfortable enough to broach the issue of the caregiver's personal beliefs. She could have asked, for example, "What do you believe? Why do the innocent suffer? Do you think my son is safe in the care of God?" If the therapist followed a middle-ground approach to the disclosure of his personal beliefs, then, rather than respond to the client's questions directly, he would have said, again, "I think it might be helpful if you were to talk a bit more about your own belief in God and suffering and how it's important to you," "It sounds like you are concerned that if my beliefs are different from yours that I might try to convince you to change them and that would not be acceptable to you," or "Maybe you are worried that I won't take your religious or spiritual concerns seriously or that it isn't safe to raise these topics in counseling."

This, as I have stated, appears to represent something of an improvement over the traditional psychoanalytic approach to self-disclosure, which stipulates that the therapist or counselor never, under any circumstances, reveal anything about his or her personal belief system to a client. But does this middle-ground approach to the disclosure of personal beliefs and values really represent a step forward? Perhaps at first sight, it appears as if the practitioner is demonstrating more interest in and curiosity about the belief system of the client. And certainly from the standpoint of empathic understanding, this would not be unimportant. It does convey a certain level of care and sensitivity to say to a client, "I value your question about what I believe because I know that it is important to you" and "I want you to know that you can trust me to respect your beliefs and to help you explore the ways in which they may be important in the work we do together." At the same time—and this is a notable weakness with any middle-ground strategy—it sidesteps the more fundamental question on the mind of the client. A client, it should be noted, would have every right to say, "That's great that you will respect my beliefs and that you will help me explore the ways in which they are important for our work together, but that isn't what I asked you. My question is about what *you* believe." A middle-ground approach is in many ways little better than the turn-the-tables strategy applied by practitioners who adamantly oppose sharing any personal information whatsoever. Viewed in this light, the therapist on the training videotape—if he had absolutely no intention of exploring the theology of his client, let alone disclosing any of his own personal beliefs—was actually doing the client a favor by stopping her before she went any further with the God talk. Maybe this was part of the ground rules established at the beginning of the treatment. The client, if this were the case, would know from the get-go where the practitioner stood in terms of exploring her core theological beliefs as well as sharing any of his own. If the practitioner had little or no interest in the client's theology nor any intention of sharing aspects of his own beliefs about God, the afterlife, and the suffering of the innocent, then it would have been completely disingenuous and patronizing to feign interest simply for the purpose of projecting empathic understanding.

In the new age of anxiety, it is important for us as caregivers to demonstrate genuine interest in the core theological beliefs of clients, even if we do not share their particular views or beliefs about God. The operative word, however, is *genuine*, a genuine interest that is an almost holy curiosity about the beliefs that sustain our clients in times of crisis and duress. But this is not all that is required of us when treating the new anxiety. What is required, if we want to treat the new anxiety as effectively as possible, is a willingness to share with clients, briefly, succinctly, and appropriately, what we believe are the issues relevant to the particular case. While treating Beth, for example, I disclosed, matter-of-factly rather than heavy-handedly, a theological view that she could compare and contrast with her own belief in divine omnipotence. To do this effectively, I had to have some idea of where she was coming from theologically. In addition to being a state-licensed mental health practitioner, I am also a certified pastoral counselor and an ordained minister, so it might seem as if I have an advantage over other therapists in terms of what to listen for when a client begins to talk theology. Moreover, I would seemingly have an advantage when it comes to being able to articulate my own theological beliefs and spiritual values, having spent many years developing the art of theological reflection. Maybe so, yet when treating the new anxiety, what is ultimately more important than a theological degree or an ordination credential is a willingness to immerse oneself in the belief system of a client and an openness to sharing one's own core theological views. The latter, of course, presupposes having a clear understanding of our own belief systems, of what forms the basis of our own meaning making.

With Beth, any psychotherapist, mental health practitioner, or pastoral counselor would be able to tell without too much difficulty how her core theological beliefs about the nature of God and the role that God plays in the world were fueling her anxiety. She was caught in something of a theological double bind: Either (a) as she heard from the television preacher, embrace God as being omnipotent and omnipresent, with the understanding that God will at times intervene to teach us a rather harsh lesson (out of "love") or (b) as Nietzsche would have it, accept that God is dead. We can see, whether we have formal theological training or not, that either extreme—the harsh interventionist God or no God at all—has the potential of triggering Beth's apprehensive expectation about the present and the future. What was needed at this point was a reframing of Beth's core theological views, which we managed to do after I first disclosed something of my own theology. Notice that I did not preach her a sermon, give her a lecture, or even tell her that a God of presence and love was my own core theological belief. Rather, I simply offered this to her as something for her own reflection: "What if God's power is the power of love, not the power of might?" and "What if God is there in the backyard with you and your friend and your children, to love you and support you and sustain you?" Later, in the interest of ethical practice, I did inform Beth that my own theological view was that God was more presence than power, which she was free to accept, reject, modify, or table for further consideration. The intervention had the immediate effect of reducing her anxiety level, and as she continued to reflect on the theology of divine presence in subsequent weeks, her anxiety became even more manageable.

It should be clear by now that I accept the view that psychotherapy, mental health counseling, and pastoral counseling are not value-free disciplines, so disclosing our core theological beliefs and spiritual values, appropriately and with great care, is ethical and it actually assists clients in maintaining their autonomy. By exposing our core values, we are less likely to inadvertently impose them onto clients; at the same time, clients will have the opportunity to examine the beliefs that we disclose, carefully and critically. As Frame (2003) argues, "confronting your own personal history with and current orientation toward religion and spirituality is critical. I believe that as counselors, one of the best tools we have to offer our clients is ourselves" (p. 1). Jones (2003), in his book *The Mirror of God*, agrees: "I am one of those people who think that the most important tool a therapist has is their self" (p. 144). As I point out earlier, psychotherapists have often taken the use of self in therapy to mean the giving of unconditional positive regard, empathic listening and care, and so forth. In a supermodern world, however, one characterized by significant change, transition, and disorientation, the use of self on the part of the practitioner must be extended to include the appropriate sharing of core theological beliefs and spiritual values. Frame puts it this way:

> In the therapeutic encounter, our humanness, authenticity, and empathy can be catalysts for change. If we are open to our own personal growth, are willing to move beyond our comfort zones, and are open to exploring what gives our lives meaning, then we are capable of being excellent role models for our clients. Likewise, if we are unaware of our own inner conflicts, have unresolved issues that are outside of our awareness, or are reluctant to confront our questions about meaning and values in our lives, we can severely limit or even harm our clients' growth process. (pp. 1–2)

In this new age of anxiety, where fear and fearmongering abound, where people try without great success to make sense of a rapidly changing world, where the traditional places of meaning making have given way to the proliferation of nonplaces, therapy becomes an essential place for helping clients discover what gives their lives authentic hope and meaning. Practitioners, however, must first be clear about what gives their own lives hope and meaning. Then and only then, after confronting our own questions about meaning, beliefs, and values, will we become the excellent role models for integrating spirituality into everyday life, specifically, everyday life in an anxious world. This is what is ultimately required of all practitioners—those very religious, the nominally religious, and the nonreligious—when treating the new post–September 11 anxiety. I would be remiss, however, if I did not address the risks involved in giving the green light to practitioners to "go there" with clients, into the spiritual world of those in our care. For example, there will always be, when working with the core beliefs of anxious clients, the potential for imposing our values and theology onto those of a different faith perspective, not to mention the nonbeliever. There is a distinct power differential between counselor and client, something that we can clearly see in the vignette from the training videotape. The therapist, despite the client's need to explore issues of a theological nature, steered her ever so subtly in a different direction, away from anything having to do with religion and spirituality. And yet, the power differential can also be misused to (a) steer clients toward theological issues when they would rather not go there or (b) steer those of another faith framework toward one that we deem more appropriate.

A Word of Caution

The remainder of this chapter focuses on the danger of imposing one's core theological beliefs and spiritual values onto unsuspecting clients. It is, to be sure, a danger that is real and one that must therefore be taken seriously. We can imagine, without too much difficulty, various scenarios where the application of one's core beliefs to the treatment of anxiety could backfire. Practitioners who embrace a set of traditional religious beliefs and values may, when working with a client who is spiritual but not religious, feel the need to point out the error of the individual's ways. In other words, the therapist or counselor may respond judgmentally to a client who is presenting unconventional or, more to the point, unorthodox religious beliefs. Maybe the therapist strongly believes that today's postmodern or supermodern individual is adrift or unmoored when it comes to spiritual beliefs and values, that spirituality without any religious or theological grounding is yet another solitary nonplace. There is plenty of justification for reaching this conclusion. The therapist would then not be entirely out of line to remind the spiritual-but-not-religious client of the need for grounding in a particular faith tradition.

In a supermodern age of anxiety, one characterized by enough solitude already, locating oneself spiritually within a core tradition becomes rather necessary for the purposes of comprehensive meaning making. The fact is that being spiritual without being religious, without having any theological framework or structure, leaves us susceptible to anxiety, especially in times of crisis when it becomes apparent that there is nothing substantive enough to support or sustain us (Jones, 2003). Frame (2003) urges practitioners to help their clients find, in terms of meaning making, a healthy balance between sufficient theological structure and the freedom of spirit. It is important, she argues, that we clearly convey to our clients that

> either too much structure or too much spirit can threaten the welfare of one's religious and spiritual lives. Despite the attempts to categorize religion by its structures and spirituality by its freedom from structures, it is evident that pure spirit is amorphous without some structure and that overly rigid structures often deaden the spirit they were designed to proclaim. (p. 8)

Put into the language of supermodernity, we could say that being purely spiritual without having any substantive theological grounding constitutes yet another solitary nonplace, hardly conducive to the development of authentic meaning and the lessening of anxiety.

Along with the need for encouraging anxious clients to have enough theological depth and grounding, practitioners, particularly, those affiliated with established religious faith traditions, must guard against being directly or indirectly judgmental about the unconventional views of those who intentionally depart from orthodox Judeo-Christian beliefs. There is the distinct possibility that religious practitioners may take what I have been saying throughout this book and apply it, almost evangelistically, to the conversion of their clients. Let me be clear: This is not what I am saying. Converting the wayward or the "lost" has no place in psychotherapy, mental health counseling, or even pastoral counseling for that matter. Exploring a client's core belief system does not give us license to manipulate the individual's religious or theological views toward our way of thinking. Rather, identifying and exploring core theological beliefs is ultimately for the purpose of understanding, empathically, what constitutes meaning for an anxious client and how that meaning is applied to various situations and events in the person's life. If we clearly see, as we did with the case of Beth, that certain beliefs are doing more harm than good, are increasing rather than decreasing the individual's level of anxiety, then we have every right to point this out to the client, albeit with compassion and sensitivity. Note that with Beth I did not judge or shame her into changing her core theological belief about the nature of God and the nature of God's involvement in the world. In fact, if she had decided at the end of the day or at the end of the counseling session to maintain her belief in an all-powerful God who intervenes directly into this world of ours, even in ways that become painful for human beings, I would have had to accept that Beth is free to construct her own belief system, even if it differs from my own. A client's belief system, as Schreurs (2002) argues,

> may be contrary to what a therapist as a trained psychologist believes to be true, but here the point is not what therapists believe. The point is that this is

the key to *understanding* spiritual people and to discerning in what ways *their* relationship with the Divine may be supportive, confusing, or obstructive to their therapy. (p. 200)

Therapeutically, then, the issue is not so much what clients believe in terms of the rightness or wrongness of their core views but rather how these beliefs function to promote growth and health or keep clients trapped in a closed cognitive system.

Granted, it can be a rather fine line between what clients believe and how these core beliefs are applied to an overabundance of national and world events. No doubt, some practitioners would think that they are focusing on how clients apply core beliefs to everyday living when, in fact, they are more interested in whether those in their care believe all the right things about God, religious faith, and the church. This is where the issue of accountability enters the picture, specifically, the practitioner's willingness to hold himself or herself accountable to a supervisor or colleague who can offer ongoing and constructive feedback. Ideally, to keep from imposing our belief systems onto anxious clients, we need the services of a therapeutic team, much like that of the Milan approach to family therapy. Realistically, however, few of us have access to a professional therapeutic team in today's world, where so much therapy or counseling takes place in the context of private practice. Still, when it comes to immersing ourselves therapeutically in the core theological belief system of an anxious client, it is important that we hold ourselves accountable and, more important, that we entrust ourselves and our work to the scrutiny of other professional colleagues. This is even more important when the issue revolves around self-disclosure on the part of the therapist or counselor, that is, the disclosure of the practitioner's personal beliefs and values. As I note earlier, no human being, not even one with an advanced academic degree, years of clinical training, and a professional license and certification, can ever be completely objective. We all have our blind spots, particularly when the issue focuses on core beliefs about ultimate reality and what we choose to ground our lives in during these anxious times. Make no mistake, addressing the core religious beliefs and spiritual values of anxious clients and disclosing our own core beliefs is something that must be done with great care, skill, and finesse.

In treating the new anxiety, one of the most effective therapeutic tools that practitioners have at their disposal is the self. This includes the core beliefs and values of the caregiver. Great care, however, is needed in terms of bringing one's self into the counseling session, particularly when the issue involves the religious beliefs and spiritual values of the therapist. History, not to mention today's newspaper, contains no shortage of vivid examples of how religion and theology can be imposed onto those who are vulnerable, less powerful, and least suspecting. At the same time, examples abound of how religion can be an authentic source of hope and healing. Thus, a certain double-edgedness is inherent in religion and theology in any time and place, including the present age of anxiety. I would even go so far as to say that religion, more than anything else, has the greatest power to hurt or heal. Applied to the new anxiety, we can modify the statement and say that core religious beliefs and theological values have the capacity to lessen or intensify the apprehensive expectation of the anxious client. It is therefore important for practitioners to understand the double-edgedness of religious belief, that it is never an all-good object or all-bad object. It all depends on how it is applied to various situations and sets of circumstances. For the atheistic therapist who closes the door on any God talk, it requires a willingness to think outside the box and avoid the temptation to regard religion as being all bad. Conversely, for the therapist who is a believer, who views religion in an exclusively positive light, it requires a willingness to develop a method of critiquing religious faith in general and one's own personal beliefs in particular. Frame (2003) puts it this way:

> One area in which counselors are most vulnerable is in placing their own needs above those of their clients. This liability comes into play in unique ways when counselors work with clients' religious and spiritual concerns. For example, counselors who are highly invested in their own beliefs could attempt to satisfy their needs to share their faith by proselytizing clients who are struggling to find a meaningful spiritual direction. Conversely, counselors who are hostile toward religion in general or toward a particular expression of religion might inadvertently discourage clients from exploring certain belief systems for fear of receiving disapproval from their counselors. For example, a counselor who was raised in a fundamentalist Christian church might have rejected this form of Christianity. As a result, he gives subtle, nonverbal cues to his clients that their views of the Bible, the role of women in the church, and their conservative social mores are unacceptable. . . . Thus, fearing rejection by their counselor, clients maintaining a fundamentalist Christian perspective might terminate counseling prematurely.
>
> Continual self-examination and personal counseling can enable counselors to increase their awareness of how they are vulnerable to placing their own needs ahead of those of their clients. Because introducing religious and spiritual material into counseling is a value-laden enterprise . . . counselors increased clarity regarding their own values reduces the likelihood that they will seek to have clients conform to their values. (p. 286)

The risk of imposing our beliefs and values onto clients highlights the need for ongoing critical reflection and self-evaluation. Some practitioners might be temped to say that we ought not "go there" in the first place into the realm of a client's core theological beliefs, let alone share any of our own. I suppose that, in one sense, the problem would be solved, but in another sense, we would be dismissing outright a vital resource necessary for the treatment of the new anxiety. The issue, then, when treating the new anxiety, is not if we will "go there" with the anxious client, exploring his or her core religious beliefs and spiritual values and, when appropriate, disclosing our own, but when and how. It is no longer feasible in a supermodern world to avoid or ignore the theological underpinnings of a client's meaning making. This does not merely apply to therapists and counselors who are nonreligious or perhaps even atheistic. I have supervised pastoral counselors who are comfortable enough discussing a client's theology, but when it comes to disclosing any of their own core values, they appear at times to be unclear about the specifics of their own belief systems. As it turns out, it is more complicated than this: My supervisees do know what they believe; yet, because of conventional psychotherapeutic paradigms that mandate keeping the self of the practitioner outside of the counseling room, they deem it inappropriate to disclose any of their theologies to a client. I myself have to guard against withholding my theology from clients, albeit for different reasons. Because of experiences that I had as a child, in the context of conservative religious settings where church leaders unhesitatingly imposed their theologies onto one and all, young and old, I purposely strive to avoid any hint of imposing my theological beliefs on anyone, especially, those in my care. In years past, I never would have intervened the way I did with Beth. The image I wanted to project was the antithesis of the intolerant image that I saw personified by religious leaders when I was a child. Yet, I needed to understand that it is not necessary to throw out the baby with the bath water, that as a pastoral counselor and mental health practitioner, I do my anxious clients little good when I approach their theologies with a hands-off attitude of "whatever's right for you." The overly tolerant approach to a client's theological beliefs and spiritual values, like the intolerant and dogmatic stance of the atheistic therapist who wants nothing to do with any God talk or the counselor who has little patience with any theology that is a departure from his or her own, is a serious obstacle to gaining clarity about how anxious clients apply their beliefs in times of crisis.

What is important to remember is that just because religion and theology can be applied inappropriately does not mean that they should be ruled out of therapeutic practice. In the new supermodern age of anxiety, overloaded, as Augé (1995) notes, with "events that encumber the present along with the recent past," people in general and our anxious clients in particular are "ever more avid for meaning." Moreover, "never before . . . have the reference points for collective identification been so unstable. The individual production of meaning is thus more necessary than ever" (pp. 29, 37). In a world characterized by the proliferation of nonplaces and the decline of religious practice, therapists and counselors will be called on more and more to answer clients' questions about the meaning and purpose of life in a post–September 11 world. In addition, practitioners will be called on to provide anxious clients with more guidance and direction, to model, as it were, a life of hope at a time when there is so much confusion and uncertainty. Therapists and counselors, working in the new age of anxiety, will need to bring all the resources of meaning to bear as they work with anxious clients. This means, for starters, keeping an open mind about the appropriate use of religious beliefs and theological values in the context of therapeutic practice. The client's core theological beliefs, as well as those of the therapist, are foundational to the treatment of the new anxiety. Helping those in our care identify the core theological frames of reference that give their lives hope, meaning, and purpose becomes an essential feature of doing therapy and counseling in an anxious world.

This, again, presupposes a holy curiosity on the part of the therapist or counselor about matters religious and spiritual. It also presupposes a willingness to clarify one's own core belief system and to use this as a resource in the treatment process. This requires great care, not to mention accountability, as we look to those who will not hesitate to give us objective feedback, who can speak to us the truth in love (e.g., a supervisor, a professional colleague, a therapist). This applies to all practitioners, whatever their levels of training and expertise. All of us, including experienced therapists and counselors, have our blind spots and our personal agendas, particularly when we are talking about core beliefs that form the essence of an epistemological framework. There can never be too much self-awareness on the part of psychotherapists, mental health practitioners, and pastoral counselors, and this applies as much to the therapist with advanced credentials as it does to the counselor in training. My own experience as a supervisor has taught me that those of us with advanced training and expertise, those of us who have been engaged in clinical practice for a number of years, sometimes have greater difficulty thinking outside the box of established frames of reference. Without the same level of supervision and scrutiny of one's work, as was the case in our earlier years of training, the therapist can habitually work out of well-established assumptions and presuppositions that are outside the realm of conscious awareness. Unless there is ongoing accountability to self and other professionals, the potential exists for imposing our way of thinking and what we believe onto those in our care.

With my students and supervisees, I emphasize developing, before learning any psychology or counseling theory and before learning any therapeutic skills and techniques, the core competency of *bracketing*. We may, after all, know everything there is to know about psychology, psychotherapy, and psychopharmacology, and yet it matters little if we have not learned to bracket our core beliefs, assumptions, and presuppositions as we work with anxious clients. Bracketing comes to us by way of the discipline of philosophy, and it means, quite literally, the setting aside of our core beliefs and values long enough to take an objective and open-minded look at someone else's point of view. In the context of caring for the anxious, this means, for example, that the overly tolerant practitioner who believes that one set of theological beliefs is as good as another would need to bracket or set aside this assumption to see that one set of beliefs has the potential to increase a client's anxiety whereas another set of beliefs can lessen it dramatically. This is illustrated in the case of Beth. The atheistic therapist would need to bracket the assumption that all forms of religion and spirituality are irrelevant, potentially harmful, or both. In so doing, he or she would see that the client's search for a harmonious relationship with God is completely justifiable and, more important, oftentimes foundational for emotional and spiritual growth. Finally, the religious counselor would need to bracket the assumption that his or her set of core beliefs is necessarily the definitive standard, that one only gets to God by way of a single religious path. In my own Judeo-Christian religious tradition, there is always the tendency to take Jesus's words in the 14th chapter of the Book of John literally, that he and only he is the way, the truth, and the life; that no one can ever hope to get to God except through his teaching, death, and resurrection. I, of course, as a practicing Christian, do take Jesus at his word, that he is the way to God for those of us who are in fact Christian. For those who follow different faith traditions, I bracket my own theological beliefs and assumptions to get a clear understanding of how others get to God and how their faith frameworks promote health, peace, and well-being or how it fuels their anxiety. The same approach is applicable with a nonbeliever, namely, determining how the client's stance of nonbelief either leads to peaceful living or to apprehensive expectation about the present and the future. Although the what of a client's belief system is indeed significant, it is how a client—whether Christian, Jewish, Muslim, Buddhist, Hindu, or nonreligious—applies his or her core beliefs to everyday living that becomes the primary focus of the therapy, especially when treating the new anxiety.

For some, it may seem as if a therapeutic modality combining cognitive therapy and theology, one designed as an intervention method with the new anxiety, is a risky proposition. There is, as I have been noting, a risk any time that practitioners disclose their theological views to clients, particularly, clients who are feeling anxious. In an age of change, confusion, and disorientation, more than a few anxious clients will be only too happy to latch onto the core beliefs of a caregiver to find some temporary relief from their anxious feelings. It is important to point out, apropos to this study, that

> cognitive therapists have been accused of indoctrinating clients with their own view of what is rational. The legitimate questions being asked include: Why should the client accept the philosophy of the therapist? What makes the therapist's view of what is true or false any more valid than the client's? Is the claim of the rightness of the therapist's view based on academic authority, professional consensus, intuition, divine revelation, scientific imperialism, rationalism, or some other philosophical foundation?

The cognitive therapist would respond by rightly pointing out that "the therapist's judgment of the truth or falseness of a client's belief is based on *the law of parsimony*. . . . At its most basic, the law means that, all things being equal, the simplest explanation is the best." Practically speaking, "when clients are looking for an explanation for their behavior, help them find the *simplest* explanation first," then help them "find the *easiest* conclusion," and, finally, help them "pick the *least* complex answer" (McMullin, 2000, pp. 425–426, 428). This I was able to do with Beth as she began to reframe her core theological belief from that of an all-powerful God to a God who is ever present and ever loving. Beth, in clinging to her belief in an omnipotent God, did not realize that she was, in cognitive therapy terms, maintaining an attachment to the most difficult conclusion and the most complex answer. Although it was certainly not her first choice, the revised core theological belief in a God of presence and love was more in keeping with the law of parsimony and, for that matter, reality as it is, instead of reality as it should be. The effect of applying a cognitive–theological approach to the apprehensive expectation of this particular client could not have been more startling: an immediate decrease in the level of anxiety accompanied by a more relaxed state, which was reinforced in the subsequent weeks and months of the treatment.

We must keep in mind that cognitive therapy, as I have noted several times, is the best available empirically based psychotherapeutic intervention for the treatment of anxiety. And cognitive therapy primarily focuses on the core beliefs of clients. In this new age of anxiety, where clients struggle to find meaning in and give meaning to a world in transition, the focus of our work must be on the core beliefs that are foundational to the client's process of meaning making. For many if not most of our clients, the core beliefs that inform their meaning making will be theological or spiritual. Thus, it is no longer optional to "go there" with anxious clients into the realm of core theological beliefs and spiritual values. Nor, I argue, is it optional for practitioners to disclose their own core beliefs and values, especially when asked to do so by an anxious client or when the counseling situation warrants such appropriate self-disclosure. Consequently, a cognitive–theological approach to the treatment of the new anxiety requires no shortage of self-awareness, self-discipline, and accountability to oneself and to others. Otherwise, "going there" with clients into their religious beliefs and theological views, as well as disclosing one's own core set of values, will be done at great risk to those in our care.

Several years ago, I was supervising Mike, a counselor in training who reported intervening with a client after she disclosed that she was feeling abandoned by God. The client, as it turned out, was worrying excessively about recent developments in the life of her family that she feared would have a negative impact for years to come. Susan, a 42-year-old wife and a mother of two teenage girls, revealed to Mike that her husband had been one of the many victims of downsizing and outsourcing with the automobile industry. Because they had faced unemployment for over a year, the couple made a decision, "after praying to God," that they and their children would relocate to another state where they would have a better life. The dream of a better life, however, has eluded them, even though they, in her words, "believed with all our hearts that this is where God was leading us." Susan's husband has not been able to find any steady employment; he works as a temporary laborer at various construction sites. The couple agreed before and after relocating that it would be best for Susan not to work full-time, in light of having two teenagers to look after. Susan does work part-time in retail but, like her husband, receives no benefits from her employer. Their credit cards are about to max out because basic monthly expenses (e.g., groceries, gas, school supplies) are paid for with plastic rather than cash. In addition, one of the daughters suffers from asthma, which means that the family has to pay out of pocket for any doctor visits as well as for any prescribed medication. A devout Christian, Susan believes that "if you go to church, pray, and live a good life, God will take care of you." Given the family's present set of circumstances, it is difficult to find, at the present moment, comfort in this core belief. What resonates with Susan more and more are the Good Friday words of Jesus from the cross: "My God, my God, why have you forsaken me?" This is what prompted her to make an appointment for counseling.

MIKE: How has the week been going, Susan?

SUSAN: I feel like we're sinking.

MIKE: Who is sinking?

SUSAN: My family. We trusted God to help us with the move. We couldn't stay where we were; there was no work. There isn't any work here either. I'm starting to feel desperate.

MIKE: Desperate about . . . ?

SUSAN: Everything! There's no work, no money. I don't know where to turn. It was so different for my parents. My father worked for the same company all his life. My mother never had to work. The world is so different now.

MIKE: Yes, it is. How are you holding up under all the pressure?

SUSAN: Not well. I can't turn it off.

MIKE: Can't turn what off?

SUSAN: Worrying. I can't stop thinking about it. I can't sleep. I feel exhausted all the time. I don't want to blame my husband, but sometimes I can't help it. We're arguing a lot.

MIKE: How is your relationship with God?

SUSAN: I don't know. Sometimes I wonder if God is even there anymore. I pray every day for help and guidance. I pray for God to help us out of this situation.

MIKE: And what do you hear God say?

SUSAN: Nothing! That's the problem. I used to believe that God was always with us, but now I'm not sure . . .

MIKE: Of what?

SUSAN: Of God! I feel abandoned. I feel God has abandoned me. Same as Jesus—God abandoned him, too.

MIKE: Yes and no. Yes, Jesus had to die, so in that sense God "abandoned" him. But don't believe for a minute that God wasn't there with him on the cross. And don't you believe for a minute that God isn't there with you and your family.

SUSAN: It's hard when there's barely enough money to pay the rent and buy groceries. We can't afford my daughter's medication. My husband had a great job and benefits. We could go out to dinner, go to the movies, buy our daughters new clothes. But not anymore. The world's changed.

MIKE: It certainly has. But you know what hasn't changed? God's love for you. You remember John 3:16, don't you? God so loved the world that he gave his only son that whoever believes in him will not perish but have everlasting life.

SUSAN: I know, I know. I'm sorry. It isn't right to doubt. I know God still loves us, but . . .

MIKE: Good. Don't doubt God's love for you, Susan. God sent his son to die for you so that you might have eternal life.

SUSAN: You're right. You're absolutely right. I'm sorry. It's just that I can't stop worrying about the future. Before, it looked so promising, but now it's really scary [*begins to cry softly*].

MIKE: Susan, just remember, God so loved the world and God so loves you. He hasn't forgotten about you.

SUSAN: I know. Sometimes it just feels that way. Sometimes it really feels that way . . .

Susan, as Mike diagnosed, was struggling with excessive worry and apprehensive expectation about the present and the future relative to the unique set of circumstances affecting her family. The worry was not necessarily disproportionate to the likelihood of certain feared events. For example, there was no health insurance to cover the one daughter's medical expenses, let alone additional medical expenses for other family members. The prospect of finding employment with better pay and benefits was eluding Susan's husband, who, except for on-the-job experience he had as an assembly line worker in the automobile industry, had no training to do other types of work. In the context of the new global economy, characterized by the outsourcing of jobs, the elimination of the pension system, and the shift from long-term to shorter-term employment, this family's future was not looking very promising. Susan's concerns were therefore legitimate and proportionate to the actual set of circumstances that had befallen her family. The family was in something of a vice grip, akin to a Sartian situation where there is no way out or, more precisely, "no exit." Mike did grasp the seriousness of the situation, prompting him to intervene in terms of assessing Susan's core beliefs about God and God's involvement in the life of her family. When it came to the treatment of the new anxiety, Mike certainly had the right therapeutic instincts. Susan's health and well-being were dependent on her finding authentic hope and meaning, which would have the capacity of keeping her anxiety in check. Thus, Mike intervened to challenge Susan's core theological beliefs by bringing into the therapeutic conversation his own core belief about the constancy of God's steadfast love. The only problem, indeed, a significant problem, was that Mike's core belief did not, at this particular moment, resonate with Susan. She was not feeling the steadfast love of God, no matter how much Mike tried to get this point across to her. Instead, what resonated more with Susan's lived experience was the feeling of having been abandoned by God, something that Mike could not or would not hear and try to understand empathically.

The preceding case vignette illustrates the danger of imposing our belief system onto clients, ostensibly for their own good but in reality out of our need to save and rescue, to be authoritative, and to feel important and powerful. Mike, in intervening sermonically with Susan, failed to see that he was imposing his belief system onto this anxious and vulnerable client who was merely accepting his theological view because she felt guilty for having expressed doubts about God's love and care. As Frame (2003) points out,

> persons with fragile egos or low self-esteem could be especially vulnerable to adopting their counselor's values because of the counselor's authority and power in the relationship. These same persons could be influenced by counselor self-disclosure precisely because they have not yet formulated their own beliefs, or because they are searching for something to value and to trust and thus they attach themselves to counselors' belief systems.

Susan, as the vignette illustrates, attached herself to the counselor's core belief, not because it resonated with her lived experience, but because she was desperate enough to trust something, anything that might offer some measure of comfort and hope to her family. "In such cases," and this is certainly true of Mike's intervention, "*exposing* one's values could inadvertently result in *imposing* them on clients" (p. 287). Mike had the best intentions, and he thought that he had made a "successful intervention," that is, until he came to see me for supervision. In our supervision meeting, I pointed out that Susan attached herself to his core belief more for his benefit than for her own. It was, in a sense, almost the reverse of my own intervention with Beth: Whereas Beth felt a tangible reduction in her level of anxiety by genuinely embracing the belief that God is more presence than power, Susan felt more anxious because the belief that Mike was offering her simply did not resonate with her lived experience nor that of her family. What Mike discovered in the supervision, which he later applied in subsequent counseling sessions, was that he would do better to give voice to this anxious client's doubt, by way of another scriptural text (Mark 15:34), which for Susan had more relevance and resonance: "My God, my God, why have you forsaken me?"

CHAPTER SIX

~

A More
Comprehensive Form of Care

On a cosmic scale, our life is insignificant, yet this brief period when we
appear in the world is the time in which all meaningful questions arise.

—Paul Ricoeur

The times, as Bob Dylan sang in 1964, they are a-changin'. He can just as
easily be referring to the present age of supermodernity. In chapter 1, I note
that Americans, much like Rip Van Winkle, have awakened post–September 11 to a world that is unfamiliar. The assumption that we are immune to
acts of terrorism, that terrorism occurs anywhere and everywhere but here,
no longer holds true. Nor is there any ambiguity when it comes to the reality of global warming. Credible scientists, in a virtual spirit of unanimity, are
warning us that the earth has surpassed the point of no return, that we must
begin preparing ourselves for the effects of long-term atmospheric change.
However, as we have seen, this is easier said than done; our thirst for and dependency on oil keeps us from developing alternative energy sources. The
irony is that by some estimates we have already peaked in terms of worldwide
oil discovery and production and are therefore on the downward slope, facing the beginning of the end of oil. But that is not all. Issues having to do
with the new immigration, pluralism, and multiculturalism confound and divide us. Many of us wonder if and how the new wave of ethnically and culturally diverse groups of people can be assimilated into the mainstream of
American society, particularly when some or, perhaps, many do not appear
very motivated to do so. And all of this is without factoring in what could

very well be the most perplexing and potentially divisive issue of all, namely, the changing landscape of American economics and employment. With a widening gap developing between economic haves and have-nots, with the gradual disappearance of the American middle class, and with more and more jobs being outsourced to other parts of the world, there is a sense that American life as we know it is now a thing of the past.

As if these current events, in and of themselves, were not enough, there are the so-called fear entrepreneurs to put us further on edge. Day after day, evening after evening, week after week, we are bombarded with no shortage of "expert" analyses, as commentators weigh in with their interpretations of these and many other potential crises. As Furedi (2005) points out, many of us believe that we are living in frightening times because other people—politicians, cable television news commentators, bloggers, health officials, advocacy groups, and so on—want us to feel that way. Politicians, for example, scare us into voting for them because they are somehow uniquely qualified to fight the war on terror, or so they claim. Nighttime cable news personalities stay in business to the extent that they can trigger our anxiety and therefore keep us glued to our television sets in general and to their programs in particular. And advocacy groups, for and against immigration, environmental regulation, and globalization, keep us ever mindful of myriad clear and present dangers that, they say, threaten to undo the fabric of American society. Every major event, argues Ferudi, becomes the focus for competing claims about what we need to fear. We as Americans will continue to feel more and more anxious as long as we let the so-called talking heads do our thinking for us, as long as we let them define us by our vulnerability. Ferudi challenges us to define ourselves not by our fear, anxiety, and vulnerability but by our capacity to be resilient and imagine more hopeful scenarios.

But as we discovered in chapter 2, imagining more hopeful scenarios in a post–September 11 world is not a simple matter. More to the point, how do we imagine a more hopeful present and future when the forces of supermodernity make it so difficult to do so? By applying the hermeneutical framework of supermodernity, Augé (1995) demonstrates that what we are struggling with in this new age of anxiety is not so much the collapse or the loss of meaning, as postmodernists have it, but rather the overinvestment in or the excess of meaning. With the overabundance of current national and world events, which the media are only too happy to bring to our attention, and with the rapid acceleration of human life and history, we are hard-pressed to give meaning to these events that appear on the television screen, the computer monitor, or the front page of the morning newspaper, events that are here today but somehow gone tomorrow. Tomorrow there will be new potential crises to report, thanks in large part to the advances in modern technology. Such technology makes possible the multiplication of national and global events on an unprecedented scale, keeping us ever mindful of what happened yesterday, what is happening today, and what might happen tomorrow and the day after. We are left dizzy by the pace of supermodern life and by the excess of information that we are expected to process. In the words of Kegan (1998), we are "in over our heads" (title of book). All of which highlights another problem inherent to supermodernity: Where and to whom do we turn to make sense of a world that seems to change more rapidly with each passing day? With the diminishment of traditional places of meaning making, most notably, the decline in religious involvement and practice, combined with the astonishing proliferation of nonplaces, we are left to ourselves to find meaning, any meaning, in these anxious times. In this new age of anxiety, as I have argued, the burden for helping people discover new and relevant meaning is placed on the psychotherapist, the mental health practitioner, and the pastoral counselor in the context of a particular place: the counseling session.

In chapter 3, I discuss the importance of defining, with greater clarity, the new anxiety. For example, what features does it share with a more generalized form of anxiety? How is it different? According to the *DSM–IV–TR*, the most basic and essential feature of GAD is excessive worry and apprehensive expectation about the present or the future. The worry, which is difficult to control or contain, is associated with certain symptoms, such as restlessness or feeling keyed up or on edge, being easily fatigued, difficulty concentrating, irritability, muscle tension, and sleep disturbance. Moreover, a generalized form of anxiety is characterized by excessive worry that is out of proportion to the likelihood and impact of the feared event. The essential feature of the new anxiety is also worry and apprehensive expectation, in this case, about the present and future states of the nation and the world. As it is with generalized anxiety, it is associated with the aforementioned symptoms. However, in contrast to generalized anxiety, the new anxiety is proportional to the impact and subsequent fallout from the feared events described in chapter 1 (e.g., global warming, terrorism). If any of these events occur in our lifetime or in our children's lifetime—and there is a very good chance that some will and that some currently are—the fallout will not be insignificant. Furthermore, the new anxiety is exacerbated not by the collapse or loss of meaning but by the intense need to give new meaning to a rapidly changing world. But, as I have noted, our attempts at finding new meaning in a supermodern world are thwarted by the proliferation of nonplaces, which give us the illusion of being grounded in a particular time and place. In this context, the counseling session becomes the quintessential place for finding new meaning, particularly if the practitioner is applying a cognitive therapeutic framework. Cognitive therapy, to be sure, with its emphasis on the core beliefs and values of the client, is ideally and uniquely suited for the treatment of the new anxiety, just as it is for the treatment of generalized anxiety.

In chapter 4, I focus on the core beliefs of clients who are presenting the new anxiety, and I discuss how in a post–September 11 world, the beliefs are oftentimes theological or spiritual. This puts us squarely within the tension between psychology and religion, historically not the most comfortable of bedfellows. Granted, the suggestion to immerse ourselves in the core belief system of clients, to "go there" unhesitatingly into the core values of an anxious individual, may strike some practitioners as being outside the bounds of conventional therapy and counseling. And this is certainly true if we situate the treatment of anxiety within the confines of traditional psychoanalytic paradigms. However, if we situate the treatment of the new anxiety within a different framework, namely, within CBT, we see immediately that there is plenty of precedent for delving into the core beliefs and values of clients. Not everyone agrees that this is inclusive of core theological beliefs, which begs the question, why not? If the theology of our clients is central to their meaning making, then by all means we are fundamentally obligated to "go there" with them and, in certain cases, even prompt them to do so. But there is more. In this new age of anxiety, it is not enough to explore the theological beliefs and spiritual values of the client and leave it at that. What is also required of practitioners in a time of confusion and disorientation, when people are searching for a relational place where they can begin to make some sense of the present milieu, is a willingness to share one's own core beliefs and values in an appropriate and empathic manner.

Finally, I acknowledge in chapter 5 that assessing a client's core theological beliefs for their efficaciousness vis-à-vis his or her anxious feelings is by nature a challenging undertaking, as is the disclosure of our own core beliefs. There are significant risks involved. Most notably, if a client's core theological views do not resonate with our own, we might be tempted to directly or indirectly convert the individual to our way of thinking. Said another way, we may find ourselves imposing our belief systems onto unsuspecting clients. This could have the unintended effect of prompting anxious clients, because of their excessive worry and apprehensive expectation about the present and the future, to latch onto our beliefs as a way of altogether avoiding their own anxious feelings. On the surface, it would appear as if the client's anxiety has been alleviated, but in reality, the individual's core belief system, foundational to his or her meaning making, would go largely unexamined. There is, then, a certain seductiveness that we must guard against, which is operative on multiple levels: An anxious, vulnerable client may be only too happy to embrace, unreflectively, the core beliefs of the "expert" caregiver, whereas the caregiver may feel a certain sense of pride in having the client acknowledge the wisdom of his or her "expert" beliefs and values. That being said, we must also guard against throwing the baby out with the bath water, by adopting a hands-off approach to religious beliefs and theological values simply because of the inherent risks involved. Nor is a middle-ground approach of deferring or deflecting clients' questions about our own core personal beliefs any better, at least not when it comes to the treatment of the new anxiety. Therapy in a post–September 11 world is, so to speak, a completely different ball game, and it necessitates thinking outside the box of conventional and traditional psychotherapeutic paradigms. Although a middle-ground approach, which demonstrates a certain interest in the client's questions about the caregiver's core beliefs without revealing anything about the beliefs themselves, would appear to be better than nothing, a compelling case can be made that in playing a sort of therapeutic game of dodgeball, we make anxious clients feel even more anxious.

Contextualizing Therapeutic Practice

In this new age of anxiety, we have, as Augé (1995) suggests, entered a world that we are only beginning to know how to look at. Situating this observation into the context of therapeutic practice, we can say that psychotherapists, mental health practitioners, and pastoral counselors have entered a new world that they have only begun to look at or, in some cases, not even begun to look at. To treat the new anxiety effectively will require more from caregivers, specifically, more precise theoretical frameworks and more comprehensive modalities of care. In other words, theory and practice need to be contextualized, with the reality of supermodernity first and foremost in mind. If we go about our work regarding anxiety as a more or less generalized phenomenon, treatable in the abstract or in a vacuum, then, in the words of Winnicott (2005), "you may cure your patient and not know what it is that makes him or her go on living" (p. 100). Indeed, we may intervene with an assortment of therapeutic skills and techniques designed to treat anxiety in general, without ever stopping to remember that the new anxiety, though sharing essential features with a generalized form, is fundamentally different in other respects.

The new anxiety is different in that it is connected to the urgent need to find meaning in and give meaning to a rapidly changing world. And yet, giving fresh meaning to the world of supermodernity is easier said than done, primarily because so much of supermodern existence is spent in the nonrelational world of nonplaces. Meaning making, though, happens to be fundamentally relational, which the Jewish theologian Martin Buber captures with his famous words "In the beginning is the relation" (quoted in Kelcourse, 2004, p. 69). From the very beginning of life, we make meaning in relation, starting with our primary caregivers. Because of the nonrelational nature of supermodern existence, reflected in the proliferation of nonplaces, meaning making has suddenly become, in the words of Augé (1995), a painful ordeal of solitude. The feeling that we are on our own to make sense of a world that we have not even begun to know how to look at will trigger more than a little anxiety even in the best of us. Thus, even while acknowledging the inherent risks involved in delving into the core theological beliefs of anxious and vulnerable clients, as well as the inherent risks involved in disclosing our own core beliefs and views, we are obligated, in the interest of treating the new anxiety more effectively, to "go there" with those in our care. To avoid going there with clients who are presenting the new anxiety, ostensibly because conventional psychotherapeutic wisdom frowns on such interventions, is to treat or even "cure" an anxious client without knowing what it is that makes him or her go on living.

This raises important questions: In the context of treating the new anxiety, what exactly is the nature of our therapeutic work? Is it, for example, imparting to the anxious client insight and knowledge? Is it the acquisition of self-soothing skills and techniques, such as guided meditation, centering, focusing, and so forth? Or is it more, in keeping with Carl Rogers, the giving of unconditional positive regard? Yes, of course, it can be any and all of these, but more is required. Relief from certain symptoms and an increased capacity to cope with the vicissitudes of human life are not unimportant, even in a supermodern age of anxiety. What is more important, however, is making sense of this new world that we have not yet begun to look at, because in many ways, we do not know how to look at it. I argue that in the context of treating the new anxiety, our therapeutic work must be transformative. Anxious clients will be transformed to the extent that they can find new ways to look at the strange new world around them and, in so doing, invest it with new meaning that is relevant and hopeful. As we have seen, the task of meaning making remains incomplete unless core beliefs—including and especially targeting core theological beliefs about the nature of God or the universe, the nature of God's involvement in the world, and the kind of world we are passing on to our children and their children—are addressed in depth and in earnest. It is, as Jones (2003) suggests, important to remember that "several studies have found that hopefulness and a sense that life is mean-ingful are essential to mental and physical well-being and are a major ingre-dient in a person's resiliency in the face of crisis, illness, and suffering." He goes on to say that

> studies consistently show that those who are able to draw comfort and mean-ing from their religion and employ some spiritual discipline regularly have lower levels of psychological distress, better adjustment, and less anxiety and depression, even when their social and economic status and their general health conditions are taken into account. . . . As a species we seem to need to know that our life is meaningful and purposeful. Research has shown that a sense of meaning in one's life is associated with more life-satisfaction and bet-ter mental and physical well-being. So these religious concepts like hope, meaning, and purpose turn out to be critical for mental and physical health and for psychological resilience and coping. (pp. 99–100)

Jones is discussing the importance of meaning making for overall life sat-isfaction. Situated in the context of the new anxiety, his words carry even greater weight. Therapy and counseling in a supermodern age of anxiety must be directed toward the transformation of the client. By this, however, he does not simply mean "transformation" in the conventional psychothera-peutic sense of the term, inclusive of "an individual's ways of thinking, feel-ing, and behaving" (p. 164). Insight, symptom removal, and the develop-ment of coping skills are certainly all well and good, and they all have the capacity to transform an anxious client's ways of thinking, feeling, and be-having. But this is as far as the transformation process goes. Even more, what is required in a supermodern age, characterized by perpetual change, confu-sion, and disorientation, is for therapy and counseling to become the context or the place for transforming the anxious individual's ways of knowing. Ther-apy in the new age of anxiety will be transformative to the extent that it can address the epistemological foundations of a client's meaning making. And as we have seen, these foundations are core beliefs that are primarily theo-logical. If, because of conventional psychotherapeutic thinking, we steer clear of the theological foundations of an anxious client's meaning making, then again, we may cure the individual through the application of insight, coping skills, and unconditional positive regard without ever getting to the bottom of what makes him or her go on living.

The discussion does not end here. Although the core theological beliefs of an anxious client are of primary importance in this new age of anxiety, so are the therapist's. The days of applying a hands-off approach to the theological beliefs and spiritual values of a client are over, or they should be over, particularly when the individual presents with the new anxiety. Moreover, I argue that the days of therapists' and counselors' withholding their own core beliefs from clients out of concern that such self-disclosure will foster inhibition or overdependence are over, too, or at the very least should be coming to a close. This brings into sharper focus the precise nature of the use of self in therapy. Heretofore, this has been taken to mean, as was pointed out in the discussion of self-psychology, an intentional empathic immersion into the lived experience of the client. Empathy, according to Kohut (as cited in Cooper-White, 2004),

> is not caring but careful perspective taking, attempting to understand the world through the inner experience and perspective of the other, as a means of gathering information about the other's needs, affects, motives, and behaviors. It is an information-gathering "empirical" activity that does establish a powerful emotional bond between people, and as such is a *precondition* for both supportive, effective mothering and therapy but is not in and of itself warmth or kindness. . . . In this sense empathy is often experienced as profoundly beneficial to patients—not because they feel warmly loved and reparented, but because they feel recognized and understood. (p. 178)

This represents a significant departure from classical forms of psychoanalytic therapeutic practice where the practitioner dispenses knowledge and insight but little else. The empathic immersion that Kohut and self-psychology have in mind calls for more intentional use of self, particularly, that of an emotional nature. Kohut sees it this way:

> The emotional reserve displayed by the classical analyst—however buttressed (rationalized) by the theory that by keeping his activities to a minimum the analyst will optimally serve as a screen for the patient's transferences—may very well have been the appropriately empathic response for patients who were overstimulated as children and therefore in need of an environment that stimulated them less. On the other hand, I believe that gifted analysts—whatever their consciously held and openly professed theoretical beliefs—have always, subtly or not so subtly, discarded their straitlaced reserve in responding to those patients who, during childhood, were deprived of the palpable emotionality of the selfobject. And they have thus provided for these patients (e.g., via the vividness of their interpretations) that minimum of emotional responsiveness without which the analytical work could not proceed optimally—just as normal mothers some decades ago continued to provide a lively emotional presence for their babies despite their lip service to the Watsonian principals of distant efficiency that had been impressed on them by their pediatricians. (pp. 170–171)

Kohut and self-psychology therefore mark an important advance in the evolution of psychotherapeutic theory and practice. To suggest that practitioners can and should bring the fullness of themselves into their clinical work was and still is revolutionary. For example, Kohut has given those of us who practice psychotherapy, mental health counseling, and pastoral counseling permission to bring not only our knowledge, insight, and expertise into the counseling session but also our emotionality. When we disclose to clients what was triggered or evoked in us as we listened to their stories, clients feel recognized and understood—and *feel* is the operative word here. Self-psychology, however, is not the only therapeutic modality to encourage the use of self in clinical practice. On the contrary, other relational therapeutic modalities, such as those put forward by feminists and theorists of object relations, all stress the fundamental importance of the use of self in the counseling process. Moreover, the impact of multiculturalism has forced the psychotherapeutic community to think well beyond the traditional bounds of theory and practice and to understand that the use of self in the form of appropriate self-disclosure is not optional with certain ethnic and cultural groups. Lee (1999) points out, for example, that when counseling Latinos and Latinas, it is important not to forget the value of *personalismo*:

> *Personalismo* refers to a preference for personal contact and individual interactions over more formal or bureaucratic dealings. . . . For the client, this would mean a preference for more personal small talk, and for the counselor this might suggest engaging in more self-disclosure and using one's first name instead of a title. (p. 95)

There is, then, plenty of precedence for bringing more of the practitioner's self into the counseling session, in the form of empathic immersion, relationality, and *personalismo*, just to name a few. More comprehensive and potentially transformative modalities of care already exist, so in that sense, practitioners have in their possession a blueprint for how to go about disclosing and sharing self appropriately in the counseling session. Unfortunately, what is often missing from the blueprint is guidance about how to encourage clients to disclose their core theological beliefs and how to disclose one's own set of core spiritual values. The matter, as we have seen, is not incidental when it comes to the treatment of the new anxiety. Although strides have certainly been made in the field of psychotherapy in terms of demonstrating more openness toward religious faith and spirituality, there still remains, on the part of some or, perhaps, many therapists and counselors, a feeling of indifference or confusion at best or outright hostility at worst.

Either of these attitudes will not be helpful in treating the new anxiety. As
Gerig (2006) points out from his own clinical training,

> I was serving as cotherapist in an internship setting. My supervisors were sit-
> ting behind the one-way mirror doing live supervision. I was gathering infor-
> mation in an intake session with a family who was presenting with an adoles-
> cent boy described as being "out of control." The mother had just finished
> commenting on how God and her church have been important sources of sup-
> port for her when the telephone rang. At the other end was the familiar voice
> of my supervisor saying, "Get your client off of the God-thing . . . he is much
> too big for our counseling room." (p. 83)

In this new age of anxiety, it is, as Frosh (2002) suggests, necessary for
practitioners to own a set of unapologetic values, "in the same way as has
characterised systemic therapists' honourable stance in other areas connected with gender and abuse." Many of us—in fact, most of us—working in
the fields of psychotherapy, mental health counseling, and pastoral counseling will have no problem giving our ascent to owning a core set of values. But
to disclose these values in the context of therapy and counseling is another
matter altogether, particularly if they are religious or theological. The time
has come for thinking outside the box of traditional and, in certain cases,
even contemporary psychotherapeutic paradigms that do not allow for or
grasp the significance of the appropriate disclosure of one's core theological
beliefs and spiritual values in the context of therapy. To treat the anxiety of
a supermodern world effectively, practitioners have no choice but to own and
appropriately disclose a set of unapologetic beliefs and values. Although cau-
tion and restraint in the disclosure of our core beliefs is certainly called for
and very much in order, it remains that the anxious client will continue to
be just that, anxious, if we feel the need to get him or her off the God thing,
let alone share any of our own views about the God thing. Frosh argues that
owning and disclosing an unapologetic set of core beliefs and values fits un-
comfortably within the framework in which many therapists operate: "We
are not supposed to take a stand in therapy on the superiority of one world
view . . . against another." Everything is relative to the core beliefs of those
in our care; at the very least, we are supposed to acknowledge, if not cele-
brate, the diversity and plurality of their beliefs and views. The problem with
the psychotherapeutic stance of nondirection and value neutrality is that this
is far too weak to respond to the anxieties of life in a supermodern world. As
Frosh (2002) sees it, in the practice of psychotherapy, especially in today's
world, "the least we can do is take a stand when the opportunity offers itself."

Why? Because, even in the face of anxiety and uncertainty, people still "strive to make sense of themselves, of others, and of their surroundings, and to symbolize these in ways which are communicable and in an important sense realistic" (pp. 115–117, 150).

Certainly, the need for addressing the core theological beliefs and values of clients extends well beyond the treatment of anxiety. In fact, I argue that a necessary component of therapy and counseling—in any time and place and with any presenting issue or disorder—is the spiritual dimension of human experience. That being said, bringing religion and spirituality into therapeutic practice is even more of a necessity when it comes to the treatment of the new anxiety, for theological and spiritual values are the basis of our meaning making. They become "central to our understanding of the mentally healthy person. Furthermore, the spiritual and religious dimensions can have either beneficial or negative repercussions in one's life" (Gerig, 2006, p. 83). This was illustrated rather clearly with the case study of Beth, in chapter 4. Her core theological beliefs, we learned, possessed a certain double-edgedness in that they initially fueled her anxiety, whereas later, after being reframed, they provided her with a genuine sense of hope and comfort. Again, there would never have been this type of therapeutic breakthrough if it had not been for the fact that Beth's core theological beliefs, as well as my own, were central to the treatment of her anxiety. Implicit in this is a willingness on the part of practitioners to be open to more comprehensive and potentially transformative modalities of care, modalities that require the intentional and unapologetic use of self in the counseling session. "I am one of those people," writes Jones (2003), "who think that the most important tool a therapist has is their self—their life experiences, their sense of humor, their empathy and compassion, their intelligence and creativity." To Jones's list, I add, apropos to this study of the treatment of the new anxiety, the core religious beliefs and spiritual values of the practitioner. Jones continues,

> Techniques, interventions, and interpretations are important, but they take place in a relational context. Beyond very narrowly defined problems like a single fear of heights or snakes, research suggests that two therapists can use the same technique and get remarkably different results. What the research literature calls "nonspecific factors"—like the quality of the relationship between the therapist and the patient—have been found to play a significant role in how successful or unsuccessful the therapy is. So, preparing the therapist is at least as important as preparing the therapeutic techniques.
>
> I think this is a lesson from the practice of psychotherapy that applies to much of life. In coping with the ever-changing currents and sudden rapids that

constitute our ordinary lives, who we are as spiritual persons is at least as important as any bits of information or particular skills we have learned. (pp. 144–145)

The emphasis on the quality of the relationship harks back to Augé's assessment of supermodernity, where the central issue becomes the creation and the fostering of a relational place in which anxious clients can be intentional about the task of meaning making. In the context of a supermodern world, that relational place is therapy and counseling. In today's world, characterized by the acceleration of time and history, the overabundance of current events and analysis of these events, the proliferation of nonplaces, an apprehensive expectation about the present and the future, and the diminishment of religious practice, therapy may very well become, if it has not already, the quintessential relational place for clarifying the nature of an individual's meaning making. Clearly, this presupposes that meaning making is most fundamentally a relational undertaking, that it must never be reduced to yet another ordeal of solitude. The issues that we face as a nation and world are extraordinarily complex and unsettling, evoking more than a little anxiety in many if not all of us. What is the meaning of it all? What do we believe about the nature of God and God's involvement in the world? Is there hope for the present and the future? Will we leave our children and their children a better world? How we answer these questions will depend, first and foremost, on what we believe. In the context of a relational place of care, practitioners who are willing to "go there" with clients into the God thing are in a position to reflect back to clients certain core theological views that may or may not be beneficial to their emotional and spiritual lives. "Theoretically, a therapist has to maintain a neutral stance but that is only true as far as it goes. One cannot make decisions about strategy, interventions, or interpretations without at some point taking a stand" (Schreurs, 2002, p. 220). In this new age of anxiety, taking a stand in therapy means helping clients become clear about what core theological beliefs bring them hope and serenity and what beliefs contribute to the perpetuation of their anxious feelings.

Treating the new anxiety effectively requires a willingness on the part of practitioners to think outside the box of conventional psychotherapeutic norms and paradigms. To be sure, it hinges on our capacity to "go there," skillfully, into the realm of a client's system of meaning making, which involves intentionally addressing the individual's core theological beliefs about God, the state of the present and the future, and what constitutes human reality in the context of supermodernity. Moreover, it hinges on our willingness to appropriately self-disclose what we believe constitutes human reality in a supermodern age. McMullin (2000) puts it this way:

> What is human reality? Which is the true picture of the sky: the view of a 10-year-old boy or the view of *Starry Night*? What is the true nature of ourselves and our clients—the mechanistic, deterministic side, or the freedom and responsibility side? When young, I would have said, "Stars are dots, and people are people. What you see is what you get." But as I got older and thought more and learned and felt more, I realized, "Stars are the universe, and people are made of star stuff. What you see is what your understanding enables you to see."
>
> Human nature is not simple. It exists in many layers that change, move, and develop constantly. The top layer is one of simple appearance—what we see when we look, what I saw when I was 10. The bottom layer is one of deep meaning and understanding—what Van Gogh painted, what we feel on a mountain meadow, what we notice about our own nature. Our experience of living in the world forges this layer. The astronomer sees spiral galaxies, quasars, pulsars, black holes, and stellar mechanics. The astrologer sees constellations and cosmic deterministic forces influencing human nature. The ship's captain sees meridians of longitude and latitude. The minister sees the creative power of God guiding humanity. In the bottom layer, we don't see what we get; we get what we see. (p. 437)

References

American Psychiatric Association. (2000). *Diagnostic and statistical manual of mental disorders* (4th ed., text rev.). Washington, DC: Author.

Augé, M. (1995). *Non-places: Introduction to an anthropology of supermodernism.* London: Verso.

Barlow, D. H. (2002). *Anxiety and its disorders: The nature and treatment of anxiety and panic.* New York: Guilford Press.

Brooks, D. (2005, August 4). Trading cricket for jihad. *New York Times*, p. A19.

Capps, D. (1999). *Social phobia: Alleviating anxiety in an age of self-promotion.* St. Louis, MO: Chalice.

Cooper-White, P. (2004). *Shared wisdom: Use of the self in pastoral care and counseling.* Minneapolis, MN: Fortress Press.

Frame, M. W. (2003). *Integrating religion and spirituality into counseling: A comprehensive approach.* Pacific Grove, CA: Thomson Brooks/Cole.

Fries with that? [Editorial]. (2006, April 13). *New York Times*, p. A-22.

Frosh, S. (2002). *After words: The personal in gender, culture, and psychotherapy.* New York: Palgrave.

Furedi, F. (2005, October 16). Fear itself. *New York Times*, sec. 4, p. 3.

Gerig, M. (2006). *Foundations for mental health and community counseling.* Upper Saddle River, NJ: Pearson Prentice Hall.

Jones, J. (2003). *The mirror of god: Christian faith as spiritual practice—Lessons from Buddhism and psychotherapy.* New York: Palgrave Macmillan.

Jones, W. T. (1980). *A history of western philosophy: The twentieth century to Wittgenstein and Sartre.* Fort Worth, TX: Harcourt Brace Jovanovich.

Kegan, R. (1998). *In over our heads: The mental demands of modern life.* Cambridge, MA: Harvard University Press.

Kelcourse, F. (Ed.). (2004). *Human development and faith: Life-cycle stages of body, mind, and soul*. St. Louis, MO: Chalice.

Kierkegaard, S. (1981). *The concept of anxiety* (R. Thomte & A. B. Anderson, Eds.). Princeton, NJ: Princeton University Press.

Lee, W. M. L. (1999). *An introduction to multicultural counseling*. Philadelphia: Accelerated Development.

Maass, P. (2005, August 21). The breaking point. *New York Times Magazine*, pp. 30–35, 50, 56, 59. (Cover: *The Beginning of the End of Oil?*)

McMullin, R. E. (2000). *The new handbook of cognitive therapy techniques*. New York: Norton.

Miller, W. (Ed.). (1999). *Integrating spirituality into treatment: Resources for practitioners*. Washington, DC: American Psychological Association.

Nuth, J. M. (2001). *God's lovers in an age of anxiety*. Maryknoll, NY: Orbis Books.

Pyszczynski, T. A., Solomon, S., & Greenberg, J. (2003). *In the wake of 9/11: The psychology of terror*. Washington, DC: American Psychological Association.

Rieff, D. (2005, August 14). An Islamic alienation. *New York Times Magazine*, pp. 11–12.

Rieff, P. (1987). *The triumph of the therapeutic: Uses of faith after Freud*. Chicago: University of Chicago Press.

Rizzuto, A.-M. (1979). *The birth of the living god: A psychoanalytic study*. Chicago: University of Chicago Press.

Rygh, J. L., & Sanderson, W. C. (2004). *Treating generalized anxiety disorder: Evidence-based strategies, tools, and techniques*. New York: Guilford Press.

Schreurs, A. (2002). *Psychotherapy and spirituality: Integrating the spiritual dimension into therapeutic practice*. Philadelphia: Kingsley.

Sue, D. W., & Sue, D. (2002). *Counseling the culturally diverse: Theory and practice*. New York: Wiley.

Tillich, P. (2000). *The courage to be* (2nd ed.). New Haven, CT: Yale University Press.

von Balthasar, H. U. (2000). *The Christian and anxiety*. San Francisco: Ignatius Press.

Winnicott, D. W. (2005). *Playing and reality* (2nd ed.). London: Routledge.

Index

~

About the Author

Kirk A. Bingaman is assistant professor of pastoral counseling and director of the Pastoral Counseling Program in the Graduate School of Religion and Religious Education at Fordham University. He is a licensed mental health counselor in New York and a fellow with the American Association of Pastoral Counselors. His previous book, *Freud and Faith: Living in the Tension*, was published in 2003.